ENROUTE RX:

Where Healing Begins With Conversation, Faith, and Community

THE CHAIR BY THE WINDOW

A Story of Healing, Faith, and Legacy

Book Two of the ENROUTE-Rx Series

Shawn E. Wells, LFD, BCCC, CGC

ENROUTE-Rx: The Chair By The Window
Where Healing Begins With Conversation, Faith, And Community

First Edition, 2026

Published by **ENROUTE-Rx**
Printed in the United States of America

ISBN: 979-8-9946309-6-9

The content of this book is intended for educational and supportive purposes only. It is not a substitute for professional medical, legal, or mental health advice. Readers are encouraged to seek qualified professionals when additional support is needed.

Scripture quotations, when referenced, are taken from the Holy Bible, New International Version, NIV, unless otherwise noted.

DISCLAIMER

This book contains themes of grief, counseling, and faith-based guidance. While the author is trained in funeral service and Christian counseling, this work is intended for educational, inspirational, and storytelling purposes only and should not replace professional medical, psychological, or pastoral care when needed.

DEDICATION

This book is dedicated to my Aunt Eva.

Your encouragement, patience, and unwavering belief in me helped carry this vision forward. Through every idea, every conversation, and every moment when I questioned the journey, you were there, listening, supporting, and reminding me to keep going. Many of the thoughts that shaped this story were spoken out loud during the long conversations we shared. Your presence during those moments helped bring this work to life.

I am also deeply grateful to my daughter, Starr.

Your strength, wisdom, and constant encouragement pushed me to continue when the process became difficult. Walking through this journey together, from studying and completing our counseling training to building the vision behind EnRoute-Rx, has been one of the greatest blessings of my life.

This book exists because of love, faith, and the people who believed the message was worth sharing.

FOREWORD

By Starr-Brianna

My dad is a multifaceted creator and businessman, someone who leads with both faith and intuition. Throughout my life, I've had the privilege of watching him grow, evolve, and step more fully into who God has called him to be. It has truly been an honor to witness.

As a young girl, some of my favorite memories with my dad were our road trips, exploring new places, discovering new experiences, and simply enjoying the adventure of being together. He has always been the funniest person I know. From his natural sense of humor to his quick wit, he carries a light that draws people in. So, seeing him step into the role of an author feels not only fitting, but inevitable.

Over the past few years, I've watched my father deepen his relationship with God and walk with a level of intention and conviction that is both inspiring and grounding. That kind of faith produces something real, something lasting. And it is from that place where this body of work was created.

One of the most meaningful parts of my journey has been witnessing our growth unfolding side by side. Together, we completed the Board-Certified Christian Counselor course and received our certificates side by side, an experience that reflects not only his commitment to growth, but his willingness to lead by example.

What you are about to read is not just written from knowledge, but from lived experience, shaped by time, refined by wisdom, and anchored in faith.

It is a gift to witness a man not only build in the world but also build within, and I am grateful to call him my father.

Warmly,

Starr

Starr-Brianna D. Wells

Scripture

"And I heard a loud voice from heaven saying,
'Behold, the tabernacle of God is with men, and He will dwell with them, and they shall be His people. And God Himself will be with them and be their God.

And God will wipe away every tear from their eyes; there shall be no more death, nor sorrow, nor crying. There shall be no more pain, for the former things have passed away.'"

Revelation 21:3–4

AUTHOR'S NOTE

Stories have always been one of the most powerful ways people understand life.

They allow us to step into moments we may never personally experience while still recognizing something familiar inside them. Grief, healing, faith, and the search for understanding are experiences that connect people across every background.

The EnRoute-Rx series was created with that purpose in mind.

Throughout my professional life as a licensed funeral director and as a counselor, I have had the privilege of standing beside families during some of the most difficult moments they will ever face. Loss has a way of revealing the emotional and spiritual journeys people carry quietly within themselves.

Those journeys rarely begin or end at a funeral service.

They continue long afterward.

They continue in conversations between husbands and wives.
In quiet moments of reflection.
In the effort to understand pain that has been buried for years.

Sunday in a Truck introduced readers to the beginning of that journey. It explored how grief, service, and faith can shape a person's calling. That story followed Tyshawn as he began discovering the deeper purpose behind helping families navigate loss.

The Chair by the Window continues that journey from another perspective.

This book explores the quiet strength that often exists behind the scenes of ministry and healing. It reflects the patience, wisdom, and compassion required to help people understand the emotional struggles they and their loved ones carry.

Sometimes the most powerful influence in a movement is not the voice standing in front of the room, but the one sitting nearby—listening carefully and guiding others toward understanding.

While the characters and events in this book are fictional, the emotional experiences they reflect are very real. Many people carry grief, trauma, and questions about faith long before they ever speak about them.

If this story encourages even one reader to begin an honest conversation, to listen more deeply, or to extend compassion to someone who is struggling, then its purpose has been fulfilled.

Thank you for taking this journey through the pages of EnRoute-Rx.

Shawn E. Wells
LFD, BCCC, CGC

TABLE OF CONTENTS

CHAPTER 1

The Chair by the Window

The house was quiet in the early hours of the morning, the kind of quiet that only existed before the city fully woke. Outside the living room window, the streetlight still glowed faintly, holding onto the last moments of night while the sky slowly softened toward morning. Inside, the warmth of the house wrapped itself around the silence like a blanket.

Starr sat in the chair by the window.

Both hands rested gently around a cup of tea that had already begun to cool. She had been sitting there for some time, watching the street outside with the calm patience that had become part of her nature. The chair had become her place. It was where she prayed, where she thought, where she allowed the weight of the lives around her to settle long enough for her to understand it.

Eva used to sit in this chair.

Sometimes Starr could still feel the presence of that quiet wisdom lingering in the room. Eva had always believed that healing started long before people spoke their pain out loud. She believed it began in quiet moments when someone simply chose to stay present.

Starr had come to understand that truth more and more each week.

From down the hallway came the soft creak of a bedroom door closing. Jaunene had already left for school earlier that morning, rushing through the kitchen with her backpack while reminding her mother that she had volunteered to help the younger children again on Wednesday night. At twelve years old, Jaunene had already begun noticing things most children her age overlooked.

She listened closely when adults spoke.

She watched the way people carried their emotions.

And without realizing it, she had slowly begun learning the same compassion that shaped both of her parents.

Starr smiled slightly at the thought.

The house had grown used to Wednesday nights. What started as a simple dinner with a few women whose husbands attended Tyshawn's empowerment group had become something else entirely. The living room had become a place where women gathered to talk about the things they often kept hidden even from the people they loved most.

Marriage.
Fear.
Grief.
Hope.

Starr didn't lead the conversations the way most people expected a leader to. She listened first. She asked careful questions. She helped the women in the room hear one another without judgment.

Sometimes the answers people needed were already inside them.

They simply needed someone to help them find the courage to speak.

The sound of tires rolling slowly over the driveway gravel pulled Starr's attention back to the window.

Tyshawn.

She sat up slightly as the truck engine shut off outside.

The front door opened a moment later, and Tyshawn stepped inside with the quiet heaviness of someone who had spent the entire evening carrying other people's pain. His tie hung slightly loose around his collar, and his shoulders sagged in the way they often did after long nights at the church.

He stopped when he saw her sitting there.

"In the chair again," he said softly.

Starr smiled.

"Where else would I be?"

Tyshawn closed the door behind him and set his keys down on the small table near the wall. For a moment he simply stood there, looking at her in the chair with the same mixture of gratitude and exhaustion that had become familiar over the years.

The ministries had grown faster than either of them expected.

The men's empowerment group at City Life Church had become a place where men finally spoke about things they had spent their entire lives hiding. Some came carrying anger they didn't know how to release. Others carried wounds from childhood that had never fully healed.

Tyshawn listened to them all.

But listening had its own weight.

He walked into the living room and sat down on the couch across from Starr.

“The group ran late tonight,” he said.

Starr nodded.

“That usually means something important happened.”

Tyshawn rubbed his hands together slowly.

“We had a few new men show up.”

“That’s good.”

“Yes,” he said quietly. “But every new face usually comes with another story that’s been waiting a long time to be told.”

Starr watched him carefully.

“You’re carrying them again.”

Tyshawn gave a tired smile.

“I try not to.”

“But you do.”

He looked down at the floor for a moment before answering.

"Some of them don't have anywhere else to take it."

Starr leaned back in the chair.

"That's why the room exists."

Tyshawn nodded slowly.

Across the room the quiet settled again.

Outside the window the streetlight flickered once before finally turning off, giving way to the full light of morning.

And in that moment, sitting in the chair by the window, Starr had no way of knowing that the story unfolding around their lives was about to grow far heavier than either of them expected.

But she would be ready.

Because healing often begins in quiet places.

And the chair by the window had already become one of them.

CHAPTER 2

The Table That Started It All

Long before the women gathered in circles at City Life Church… before the fellowship hall filled with quiet conversations and cups of tea… before the ministry had a name…

There was simply a table.

The kitchen table in Starr's house had always been a place where people stayed longer than they intended. It sat near the window where the afternoon sun filtered through the curtains and warmed the wood across the surface. The table had seen many ordinary moments of life.

Homework spread across its surface.

Dinner plates stacked beside glasses of sweet tea.

Bills waiting to be sorted.

Jaunene coloring quietly while her parents talked about the day.

It was not a large table. But it was large enough for a few people to sit close and speak honestly.

Starr had always liked that about it.

The closeness made it difficult for anyone to pretend.

It made conversation real.

But on one particular evening, without anyone planning it, that ordinary kitchen table became something far greater than a place for meals.

It became the beginning of a ministry.

The story actually began outside City Life Church on a Wednesday evening.

At that time the men's empowerment group had only been meeting for a few weeks. The group itself had started quietly, almost accidentally. Tyshawn had noticed that many of the men he encountered through his work at the funeral home carried stories they had never shared with anyone.

Stories of loss.

Stories of childhood pain.

Stories of pressure that came with trying to be strong for everyone else.

So one evening he invited a few of them to sit down and talk.

At first the meetings were small.

Five men.

Sometimes six.

They sat in folding chairs arranged in a loose circle inside one of the classrooms at the church.

The conversations were awkward in the beginning.

Men were not accustomed to speaking openly about the parts of life that hurt.

Sometimes several minutes passed before anyone said a word.

Other times someone made a joke to ease the tension.

But week by week something slowly began changing.

They kept coming back.

And eventually the silence broke.

Outside the church building, however, something else was happening.

Several wives often waited while the meetings took place.

Some sat quietly in their cars scrolling through their phones.

Others leaned against the sides of their vehicles talking beneath the glow of the parking lot lights.

One evening Danielle stepped out of her car and noticed Starr standing near the church entrance.

"Is Tyshawn still inside?" she asked.

Starr nodded.

"They've been talking longer than usual tonight."

Danielle let out a slow breath and leaned against the side of her car.

"Marcus came home last week talking about feelings."

Starr smiled softly.

"That must have surprised you."

Danielle laughed quietly.

"You have no idea."

Another woman nearby overheard the conversation.

"My husband did the same thing," she said as she stepped closer.

"I thought something was wrong with him."

A small group began forming naturally.

Women who had been sitting quietly in their cars joined the conversation.

Each of them had noticed something similar happening in their homes.

Their husbands were talking differently.

Thinking more deeply.

Sometimes even apologizing for things they had never acknowledged before.

One woman folded her arms.

"I'm not complaining," she said. "But I honestly don't know what they're talking about in that room."

Danielle nodded.

"Marcus said they're discussing things from their childhood."

Another woman raised her eyebrows.

"My husband hasn't talked about his childhood in fifteen years."

The women laughed softly together.

For a few minutes they stood beneath the parking lot lights sharing the same quiet confusion.

Their husbands were changing.

But none of them fully understood why.

After a moment Starr looked around at the group.

"Instead of standing out here every week," she said gently, "why don't you all come by the house sometime?"

The women looked at one another.

Danielle tilted her head.

"For what?"

"Just to talk."

Another woman shrugged.

"I'd like to understand what's happening to my husband."

A third woman added quietly, "Me too."

Starr smiled.

"Then come by next Wednesday."

The following week a few women arrived at Starr's house just before the men's meeting started at the church.

The atmosphere felt casual.

No one brought anything special.

Just curiosity.

Starr poured coffee while the women settled into their chairs around the kitchen table.

At first the conversation remained light.

They talked about their children.

Work schedules.

The small routines that filled their daily lives.

But eventually the question surfaced.

"What exactly are the men talking about in that room?"

The table grew quiet.

Starr thought for a moment before answering.

“They’re talking about things they’ve carried for a long time.”

“Like what?” Danielle asked.

“Pain.”

“Fear.”

“Regret.”

The women listened carefully.

“Men aren’t usually given many places where they feel safe enough to talk honestly,” Starr continued.

“So when they finally find one… a lot of things begin coming out.”

Another woman frowned slightly.

“My husband told me something about his childhood last week that I had never heard before.”

Starr nodded.

“That happens when people begin unpacking old wounds.”

The women leaned forward.

“What are we supposed to do with that?” someone asked.

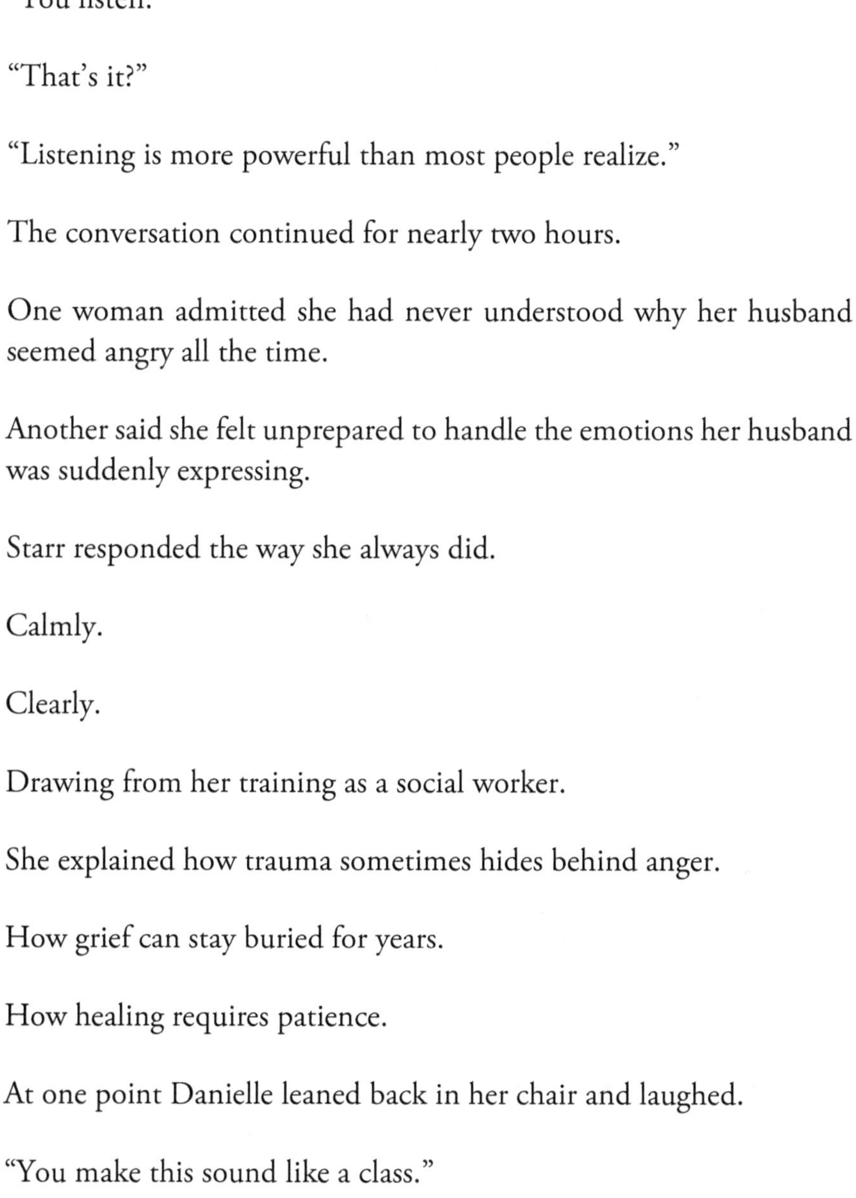

Starr smiled gently.

"You listen."

"That's it?"

"Listening is more powerful than most people realize."

The conversation continued for nearly two hours.

One woman admitted she had never understood why her husband seemed angry all the time.

Another said she felt unprepared to handle the emotions her husband was suddenly expressing.

Starr responded the way she always did.

Calmly.

Clearly.

Drawing from her training as a social worker.

She explained how trauma sometimes hides behind anger.

How grief can stay buried for years.

How healing requires patience.

At one point Danielle leaned back in her chair and laughed.

"You make this sound like a class."

Starr shook her head.

"I'm just explaining what I know."

Another woman looked around the table thoughtfully.

"We should do this again."

Several voices agreed immediately.

"Yes."

"Next week."

"And maybe we should bring food next time," someone suggested.

That idea spread quickly.

The following Wednesday someone arrived with a casserole.

Another brought dessert.

Someone else carried a container of homemade soup.

Soon the kitchen table looked like a small potluck gathering.

But the food wasn't the most important part.

The conversations continued growing deeper.

The women asked questions.

Shared frustrations.

Admitted fears.

And little by little something unexpected began happening.

They started understanding their husbands better.

One evening Danielle looked across the table at Starr.

"You should lead this."

Starr shook her head quickly.

"I'm not trying to lead anything."

"But you're the one explaining everything," Danielle said.

Another woman nodded.

"You help us understand what the men are going through."

Starr looked around the table.

"I'm just talking."

But the women had already realized something she had not.

Her voice brought clarity to confusion.

Her calm presence created safety.

Without trying, she had become the one they trusted to guide the conversation.

Weeks passed.

The group continued growing.

Soon the kitchen table was no longer large enough.

Chairs filled the living room.

Children gathered in the hallway while their mothers talked.

Jaunene often sat among them drawing pictures and listening quietly to the conversations drifting from the other room.

Eventually Pastor Barrett heard about the gatherings.

One Sunday afternoon he approached Starr after church.

"I hear something interesting has been happening at your house on Wednesday nights."

Starr smiled modestly.

"We've just been talking."

The pastor nodded thoughtfully.

"That's usually where real ministry begins."

A few weeks later he suggested moving the meetings to the church fellowship hall.

"There are more women who could benefit from those conversations," he said.

But none of them ever forgot where it began.

Around a kitchen table.

With coffee.

A few casseroles.

And a group of women simply trying to understand the men they loved.

That night the ministry was born.

Not from a program.

Not from a plan.

But from a conversation.

CHAPTER 3

Marcus

Marcus had not planned on coming to the meeting.

In fact, he had spent most of that Wednesday afternoon convincing himself that he wouldn't.

He sat in his truck outside the warehouse where he worked, the engine running quietly while the radio played a song he barely heard. The day had been long, the kind of day where every small frustration seemed heavier than usual.

The supervisor had been on edge all morning.

Orders were behind schedule.

Two employees had called in sick.

By lunchtime Marcus already felt the familiar tightness building in his chest.

It wasn't anger exactly.

It was something deeper.

Pressure.

The kind that builds slowly over years.

Pressure to provide.

Pressure to be strong.

Pressure to never show weakness.

Marcus had been carrying that pressure most of his life.

His father believed a man handled problems alone.

“Talking about your feelings don’t fix nothing,” he used to say.

So Marcus learned early how to stay quiet.

When his father drank too much.

When money ran short.

When arguments filled the house late into the night.

Silence became survival.

By the time Marcus reached adulthood, silence felt natural.

Even with Danielle.

She loved him deeply, and he loved her the same way, but there were parts of his life he had never spoken out loud.

Not because he didn’t trust her.

But because he didn’t know how to explain the weight he carried.

A week earlier Danielle had mentioned something about Tyshawn's group at the church.

"You should go," she said one evening while washing dishes.

Marcus shrugged.

"What for?"

"To talk."

He laughed softly.

"Talk about what?"

Danielle dried her hands and looked at him seriously.

"Whatever it is you keep carrying."

Marcus changed the subject.

But the conversation stayed in his mind.

Now he sat in the truck watching the afternoon traffic pass the warehouse parking lot.

The church meeting started in about an hour.

He could go home instead.

Eat dinner.

Watch television.

Pretend everything was fine.

But something inside him felt restless.

He reached for his phone and stared at the screen for a moment before texting Danielle.

You still think I should try that group tonight?

Her reply came almost immediately.

Yes.

Marcus stared at the word for a moment.

Then he sighed, turned off the engine, and started the truck again.

The drive to City Life Church took fifteen minutes.

The building looked quiet when he pulled into the parking lot. A few cars were already parked near the entrance.

Marcus sat in the truck for another minute.

His hands rested on the steering wheel.

"Just go in," he muttered to himself.

Inside the church hallway the lights were bright and welcoming.

He could hear voices coming from one of the classrooms.

Marcus followed the sound.

When he stepped into the room, several men were already sitting in a circle of chairs.

Tyshawn stood near the window speaking quietly with another man.

When he noticed Marcus standing in the doorway, he smiled.

“Come on in.”

Marcus nodded awkwardly.

“First time?” Tyshawn asked.

“Yeah.”

“Grab a chair.”

Marcus sat down slowly.

For a few minutes the room remained quiet while the rest of the group arrived.

Some men looked nervous.

Others stared at the floor.

One man cracked a joke about the uncomfortable silence.

The group laughed lightly.

Finally Tyshawn leaned forward in his chair.

“Before we start,” he said calmly, “there’s only one rule here.”

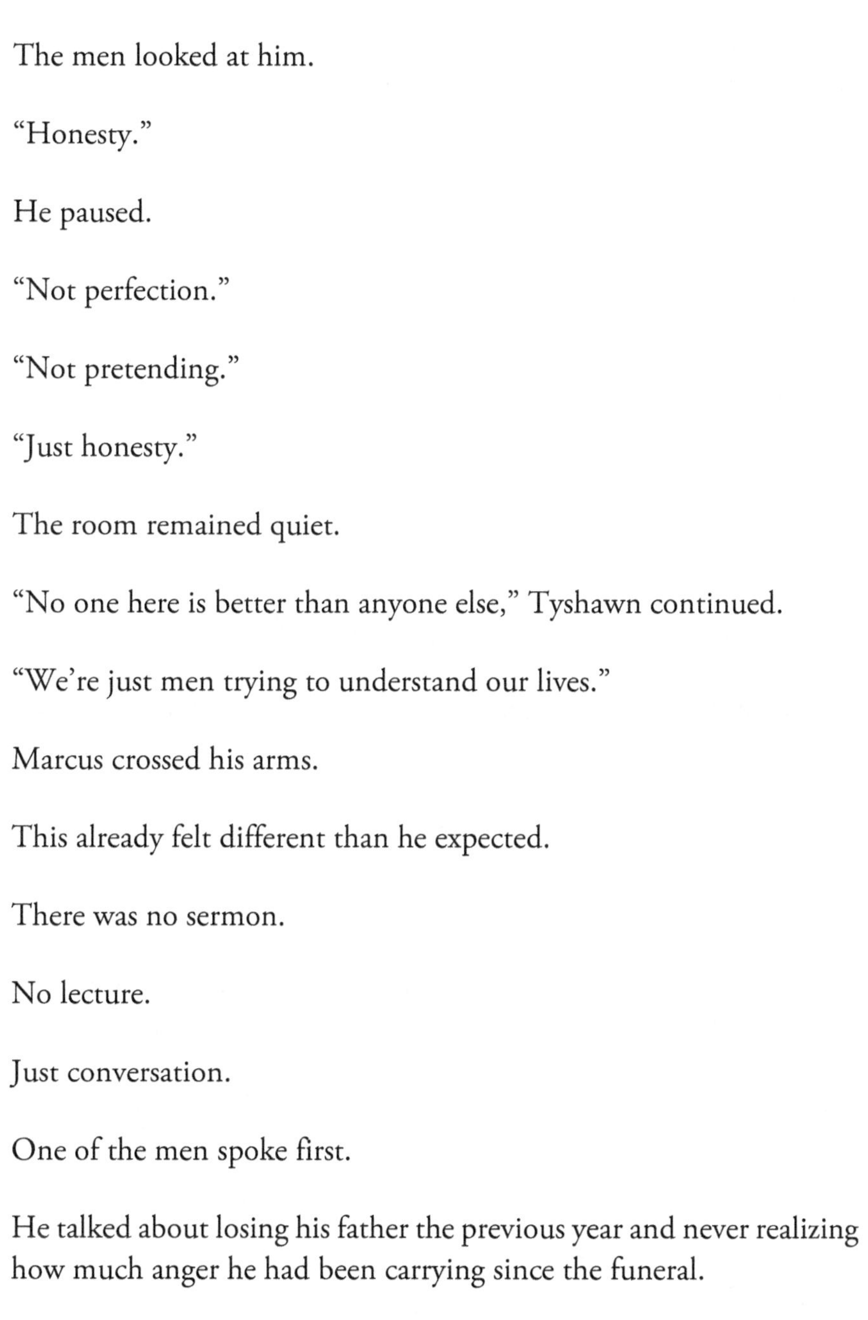

The men looked at him.

"Honesty."

He paused.

"Not perfection."

"Not pretending."

"Just honesty."

The room remained quiet.

"No one here is better than anyone else," Tyshawn continued.

"We're just men trying to understand our lives."

Marcus crossed his arms.

This already felt different than he expected.

There was no sermon.

No lecture.

Just conversation.

One of the men spoke first.

He talked about losing his father the previous year and never realizing how much anger he had been carrying since the funeral.

Another man admitted he struggled to talk to his teenage son because he didn't know how to explain his own childhood.

The stories began slowly.

But once they started, they did not stop.

Marcus listened.

He did not speak.

But he listened carefully.

And for the first time in years, he realized something surprising.

He was not the only man carrying things he had never said out loud.

Across town, at that very same moment, Danielle sat at Starr's kitchen table with the other women.

She had no idea what Marcus was hearing inside that room.

But something inside her hoped it might help him.

Back at the church, Tyshawn noticed Marcus had been quiet the entire evening.

As the meeting ended, the men began standing and gathering their jackets.

Marcus headed toward the door.

"Marcus."

He turned.

Tyshawn smiled.

“You don’t have to talk the first night.”

Marcus nodded.

“I figured that.”

“But if you come back,” Tyshawn continued, “you might find something helpful here.”

Marcus looked around the room.

The chairs were empty now.

But the conversations that had filled them still lingered in the air.

He shrugged slightly.

“Maybe.”

As he stepped outside into the cool night air, Marcus noticed the parking lot lights shining across the pavement.

He took a slow breath.

Something about the meeting felt unfamiliar.

But also strangely relieving.

For the first time in a long time, Marcus felt like he might have found a place where silence was no longer required.

And though he didn't know it yet, that decision to walk through the church doors would eventually change far more than his own life.

CHAPTER 4

The Call

The weeks after Marcus's first meeting passed quietly, but something inside him had begun to shift.

He still woke up early each morning and drove to the warehouse like he had for years. The same steel doors rolled open. The same forklifts moved pallets across the concrete floors. The same supervisors barked orders from clipboards as the workday began.

On the outside, nothing had changed.

But Marcus had started thinking more.

Listening more.

Not just at work, but at home.

Danielle noticed it first.

One evening she stood at the stove stirring a pot of soup when Marcus walked into the kitchen after work.

"How was the group tonight?" she asked.

Marcus shrugged as he opened the refrigerator.

"It was alright."

"That's all you're going to say?"

He closed the refrigerator and leaned against the counter.

"They just talk."

Danielle turned to face him.

"And?"

Marcus paused.

"And some of it makes sense."

That answer alone told her something important.

For years Marcus had avoided conversations about feelings, about the past, about anything that required emotional honesty.

Now he was listening.

The following Wednesday Marcus returned to the meeting again.

And the week after that.

Each time he spoke a little more.

Not everything.

But enough to feel the weight shifting slightly.

One evening he told the group about his father's temper.

Another week he spoke about the pressure he felt trying to provide for his family.

The other men listened without judgment.

Tyshawn guided the conversation carefully, asking questions that helped the men think more deeply about what they were carrying.

But healing is rarely a straight road.

Some weeks Marcus left the meetings feeling lighter.

Other weeks the conversations stirred memories he had buried for years.

One particular Wednesday evening, Marcus sat quietly during the entire meeting.

Tyshawn noticed.

After the group ended, he approached Marcus near the doorway.

“You alright?”

Marcus rubbed his hands together nervously.

“Just thinking.”

“About what?”

Marcus looked toward the empty chairs.

“About how much stuff I’ve been carrying.”

Tyshawn nodded.

“That’s usually the first step.”

Marcus sighed.

“Feels like too much sometimes.”

“Then take it one piece at a time,” Tyshawn said gently.

Marcus nodded, but his eyes carried a heaviness that Tyshawn recognized.

Later that night Marcus drove home in silence.

The house was quiet when he arrived.

Danielle had already gone to bed.

Marcus sat at the kitchen table for a while staring at the wood grain beneath his hands.

The house felt peaceful.

But his mind would not rest.

Memories continued surfacing.

Arguments from years earlier.

Moments he wished he could undo.

Words he had never said.

The following weeks brought more pressure.

Work became more demanding.

Overtime hours stretched late into the evening.

One afternoon Marcus received a warning from his supervisor about falling behind on production targets.

He tried to explain that the equipment had been malfunctioning.

But the supervisor dismissed the explanation.

“Excuses don’t move product,” the man said sharply.

Marcus left the office feeling humiliated.

That evening he sat in his truck outside the church before the meeting started.

The parking lot lights reflected across the windshield.

He gripped the steering wheel tightly.

Part of him wanted to walk inside.

Another part wanted to drive away.

Eventually he stepped out of the truck and entered the building.

The group gathered as usual.

Chairs arranged in a circle.

Quiet greetings.

A few tired smiles.

But Marcus remained silent that night.

After the meeting ended, he left quickly without speaking to anyone.

Danielle noticed the difference when he arrived home.

"You didn't stay long tonight," she said gently.

Marcus shrugged.

"Just tired."

She studied his face carefully.

"Something bothering you?"

"No."

But the answer came too quickly.

Danielle had learned over the years that Marcus often tried to protect her from the weight he carried.

Still, something about his voice worried her.

"Marcus," she said softly.

"You know you don't have to carry everything by yourself."

Marcus looked down at the floor.

"I know."

But knowing and believing were two different things.

Over the next several days, Marcus grew quieter.

The pressures at work continued building.

Bills arrived in the mail.

Sleep became harder.

One evening Danielle found him sitting alone in the living room staring at the television without really watching it.

She sat beside him.

"Talk to me."

Marcus shook his head slightly.

"I'm alright."

But the heaviness in his eyes told a different story.

Later that night Danielle sent a short message to Tyshawn.

Marcus seems different lately.

Tyshawn read the message carefully.

He had noticed the same thing.

Marcus had begun opening doors inside himself that had been closed for years.

Sometimes when those doors open, the pain behind them comes out all at once.

Tyshawn responded.

Keep encouraging him to come to the meetings.

He's not alone.

Danielle read the message and nodded quietly.

She hoped that was true.

But neither of them knew how close Marcus was to reaching a breaking point.

The phone call came late one night.

Tyshawn had just finished reviewing notes in his office when his phone rang.

He answered quickly.

"Hello?"

The voice on the other end trembled.

"Tyshawn… it's Danielle."

He sat upright.

“What’s wrong?”

There was a pause.

Then the words came through tears.

“Marcus is gone.”

CHAPTER 5

Marcus's Funeral

The news spread through City Life Church quietly at first.

A phone call to one member.

A message to another.

By the time the sun rose the next morning, most of the congregation already knew.

Marcus was gone.

Tyshawn sat alone in his office at the funeral home when the reality of the words finally settled into his chest. The room around him felt strangely still. Papers rested neatly on the desk in front of him. The soft hum of the air conditioner filled the silence.

He had received calls like Danielle's before.

Too many times.

But this one felt different.

Marcus had been sitting in that circle only a few weeks earlier.

Listening.

Trying.

Opening doors that had been closed most of his life.

Tyshawn lowered his head into his hands.

The familiar question crept into his thoughts.

Did I miss something?

Funeral directors learn quickly that grief often carries unanswered questions. But ministers and counselors sometimes struggle even more when those questions come.

Could he have said something different?

Could he have noticed something sooner?

Across town, Danielle sat at her kitchen table surrounded by family members who had come to support her. The house felt full, yet strangely quiet at the same time.

Marcus's brother sat in the living room speaking softly with one of Danielle's cousins.

A neighbor brought a casserole that rested untouched on the counter.

Danielle stared at the coffee cup in front of her.

Her hands trembled slightly as she held it.

There had been signs.

Now she saw them clearly.

The late nights.

The quiet moments.

The distant look in his eyes.

But in the middle of those memories, she also remembered something else.

Marcus tried.

He had walked through the doors of that church.

He had sat in the circle.

He had started speaking.

A knock came at the front door.

Danielle looked up.

When she opened it, Tyshawn stood on the porch.

Neither of them spoke at first.

Then Danielle stepped forward and embraced him tightly.

For a moment they both stood there in silence.

"I'm so sorry," Tyshawn said softly.

Danielle nodded against his shoulder.

"I know."

He followed her inside and sat at the kitchen table across from her.

"This is my fault," she whispered suddenly.

Tyshawn shook his head immediately.

"No."

"I should have noticed sooner."

"You loved him," Tyshawn said gently.

"That's what you did."

Danielle wiped her eyes.

"He was trying so hard."

"I know."

They sat quietly for several minutes.

Finally, Danielle looked at him.

"Will you handle the funeral?"

Tyshawn nodded slowly.

"Yes."

The service will be held at City Life Church.

When Tyshawn returned to the funeral home later that afternoon, he began preparing the arrangements with the careful attention he had given every family for years.

But this service required more.

Marcus had not just been another member of the community.

He had been one of the men in the circle.

One of the men searching for healing.

Tyshawn sat with Danielle later that evening in the arrangement room at the funeral home.

The soft lighting made the room feel peaceful despite the difficult conversation.

“Marcus always loved music,” Danielle said quietly.

“Did he have a favorite song?” Tyshawn asked.

She thought for a moment.

“He used to play a gospel song in the truck all the time.”

“What song?”

“Never Would Have Made It.”

Tyshawn nodded.

“That’s a good one.”

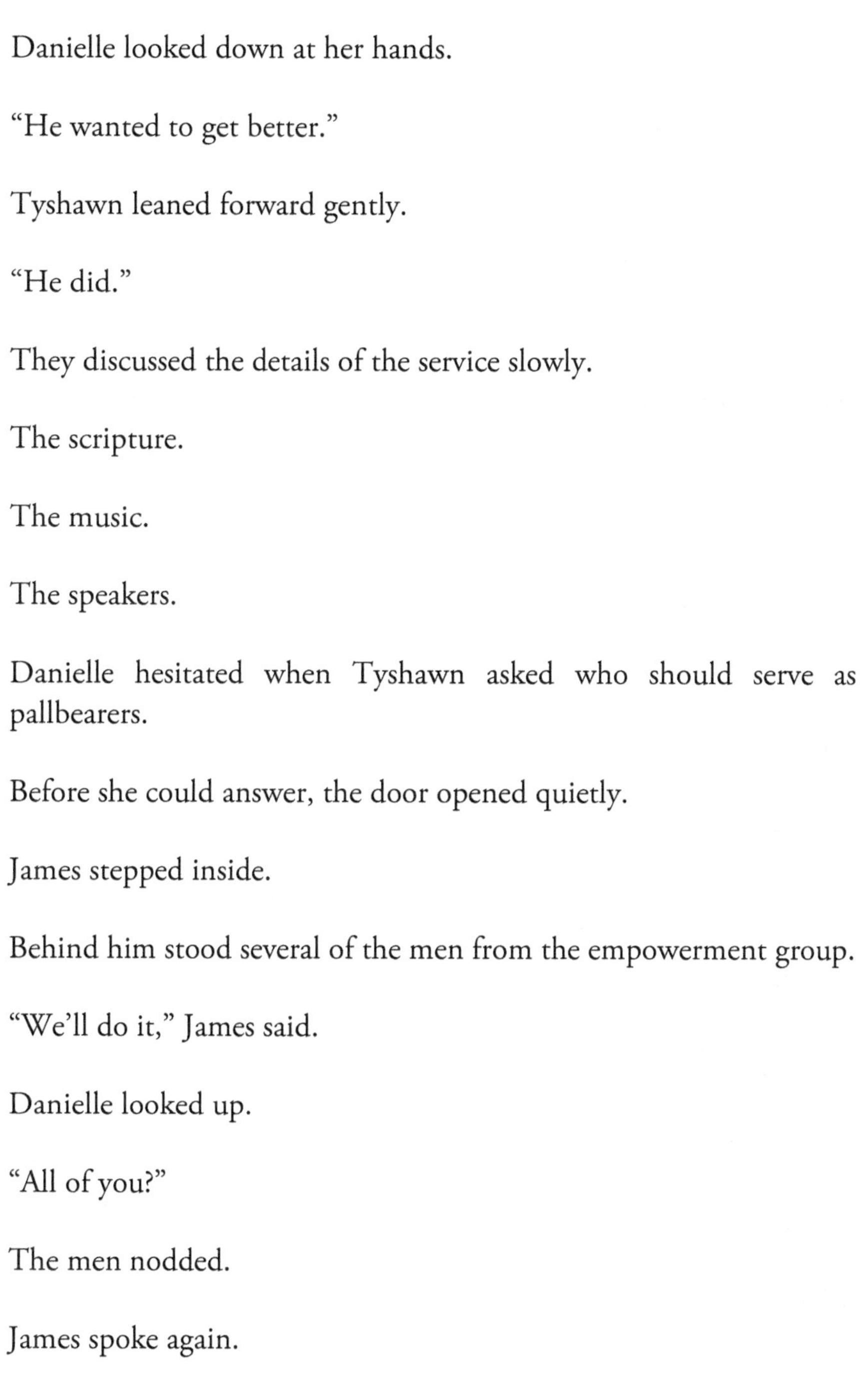

Danielle looked down at her hands.

"He wanted to get better."

Tyshawn leaned forward gently.

"He did."

They discussed the details of the service slowly.

The scripture.

The music.

The speakers.

Danielle hesitated when Tyshawn asked who should serve as pallbearers.

Before she could answer, the door opened quietly.

James stepped inside.

Behind him stood several of the men from the empowerment group.

"We'll do it," James said.

Danielle looked up.

"All of you?"

The men nodded.

James spoke again.

"Marcus sat in that circle with us."

"We'll carry him."

The day of the funeral arrived beneath gray clouds that hung low above the church.

Cars filled the parking lot early.

Members of the congregation gathered quietly in the sanctuary.

The casket rested at the front beneath a simple arrangement of white flowers.

Tyshawn stood near the front doors greeting people as they arrived.

Many of the men from the empowerment group entered together.

They wore dark suits and solemn expressions.

But they did not sit apart from their wives.

Instead, they sat together.

Side by side.

Husband and wife.

Support beside support.

The choir began the opening hymn softly.

Many people sang through tears.

When the song ended, Tyshawn stepped forward to the pulpit.

He looked out across the congregation.

Grief filled the room.

But so did love.

"Marcus was a man who wanted to be better," Tyshawn began quietly.

"He wanted to understand himself."

"He wanted to be the husband his family deserved."

His voice remained steady, but his heart felt heavy.

"He walked through the doors of this church searching for healing."

Tyshawn paused.

"And that courage should never be forgotten."

After the service ended, the pallbearers stepped forward.

The men from the empowerment group surrounded the casket.

One by one they placed their hands against the polished wood.

A circle of men.

Not just carrying a casket.

Honoring a brother.

The congregation stood silently as the casket was lifted.

Outside the church, the wind moved gently through the trees.

Tyshawn watched as the hearse door closed.

He had directed hundreds of funerals.

But this one stayed with him longer.

Because sometimes the hardest part of helping people heal…

is accepting that you cannot save everyone.

And that truth would stay with Tyshawn long after the church doors closed that day.

CHAPTER 6

The Weight of Helping

The days after Marcus's funeral felt unusually quiet.

City Life Church returned to its normal rhythm, but something had changed beneath the surface. The conversations in the hallway were softer. The laughter between friends was gentler. Even the Wednesday meetings carried a deeper tone.

Loss had a way of doing that.

It slowed people down.

Tyshawn noticed it immediately.

On Wednesday evening the men gathered again in the same classroom where Marcus had once sat quietly in the circle. The chairs were arranged the same way they always were. The fluorescent lights hummed softly above them. A few men spoke quietly as they waited for the meeting to begin.

But the empty chair remained noticeable.

No one mentioned it at first.

Finally, James spoke.

"Feels strange tonight."

The other men nodded.

Tyshawn leaned forward slightly in his chair.

"Marcus was part of this group," he said calmly. "It's alright to say his name."

For a moment the room remained quiet.

Then one of the younger men spoke.

"I keep thinking about something he said a few weeks ago."

"What was that?" Tyshawn asked.

"He said it felt like he'd been carrying things alone for years."

The man rubbed his hands together nervously.

"I didn't realize how serious he meant it."

Tyshawn nodded slowly.

"Sometimes when people begin opening those doors, the emotions behind them can feel overwhelming."

James sighed.

"I keep wondering if we should have noticed something sooner."

Tyshawn understood the feeling well.

"Everyone in this room showed Marcus something important," he said gently.

"What?"

"That he wasn't alone."

The men sat quietly reflecting on that thought.

After a few minutes Tyshawn spoke again.

"One thing we have to remember is this—healing is a process."

"Sometimes people take steps forward."

"Sometimes they struggle."

"And sometimes the pain they carry runs deeper than anyone realizes."

The room remained still.

One of the men wiped his eyes quietly.

"I wish we had more time with him."

Tyshawn nodded.

"Me too."

The conversation that night moved slowly.

Some men shared memories of Marcus.

Others talked about their own fears.

For the first time since the group began, several of them admitted something openly.

They were afraid of facing their own pain.

But something else happened that night, too.

They stayed.

No one left early.

No one avoided the conversation.

Instead, they leaned into it.

Across town, the women gathered once again at Starr's house.

The atmosphere in the living room carried the same heaviness.

Danielle sat quietly near the window while the other women spoke softly around her.

Starr poured tea into several cups before sitting beside her.

"How are you holding up?" Starr asked gently.

Danielle shrugged.

"I keep replaying everything."

"That's normal."

"I keep wondering if I missed something."

Starr placed her hand gently over Danielle's.

"When someone we love is hurting, we always wish we could see the pain sooner."

Danielle nodded slowly.

"But Marcus did something important," Starr continued.

"What?"

"He tried."

The women around the room listened quietly.

"He walked into that church looking for help."

"And that took courage."

Danielle wiped her eyes.

"I just wish he could have stayed."

Starr looked around the room.

"His story is going to help someone else."

Danielle looked up.

"How?"

"Because now we understand how serious these struggles can be."

Starr's voice remained calm but firm.

"Sometimes healing requires more than just courage. It requires support from every direction."

The women nodded thoughtfully.

Back at the church, Tyshawn locked the classroom door after the men's meeting ended.

The hallway was quiet.

Most of the congregation had already gone home.

He walked slowly through the sanctuary and sat in the front pew.

For several minutes he stared at the pulpit.

Marcus's funeral had forced him to face something difficult.

Helping people carry weight.

The stories.

The grief.

The pain that men revealed during those meetings.

Tyshawn felt responsible for all of it.

Sometimes the weight felt manageable.

Other times it felt overwhelming.

He leaned forward, resting his elbows on his knees.

“Lord,” he whispered softly.

“Help me carry this.”

The sanctuary remained silent.

But in that silence Tyshawn remembered something Pastor Barrett had once told him.

“Ministry doesn’t mean you carry people’s pain for them.”

“It means you walk beside them while they carry it themselves.”

Tyshawn sat back slowly.

The words settled into his thoughts.

He couldn’t save everyone.

But he could continue walking beside those who needed help.

And sometimes that was enough.

When he returned home later that night, the house was quiet.

Starr sat in the chair by the window with a book resting in her lap.

She looked up as he entered.

“How did the meeting go?”

Tyshawn sat down across from her.

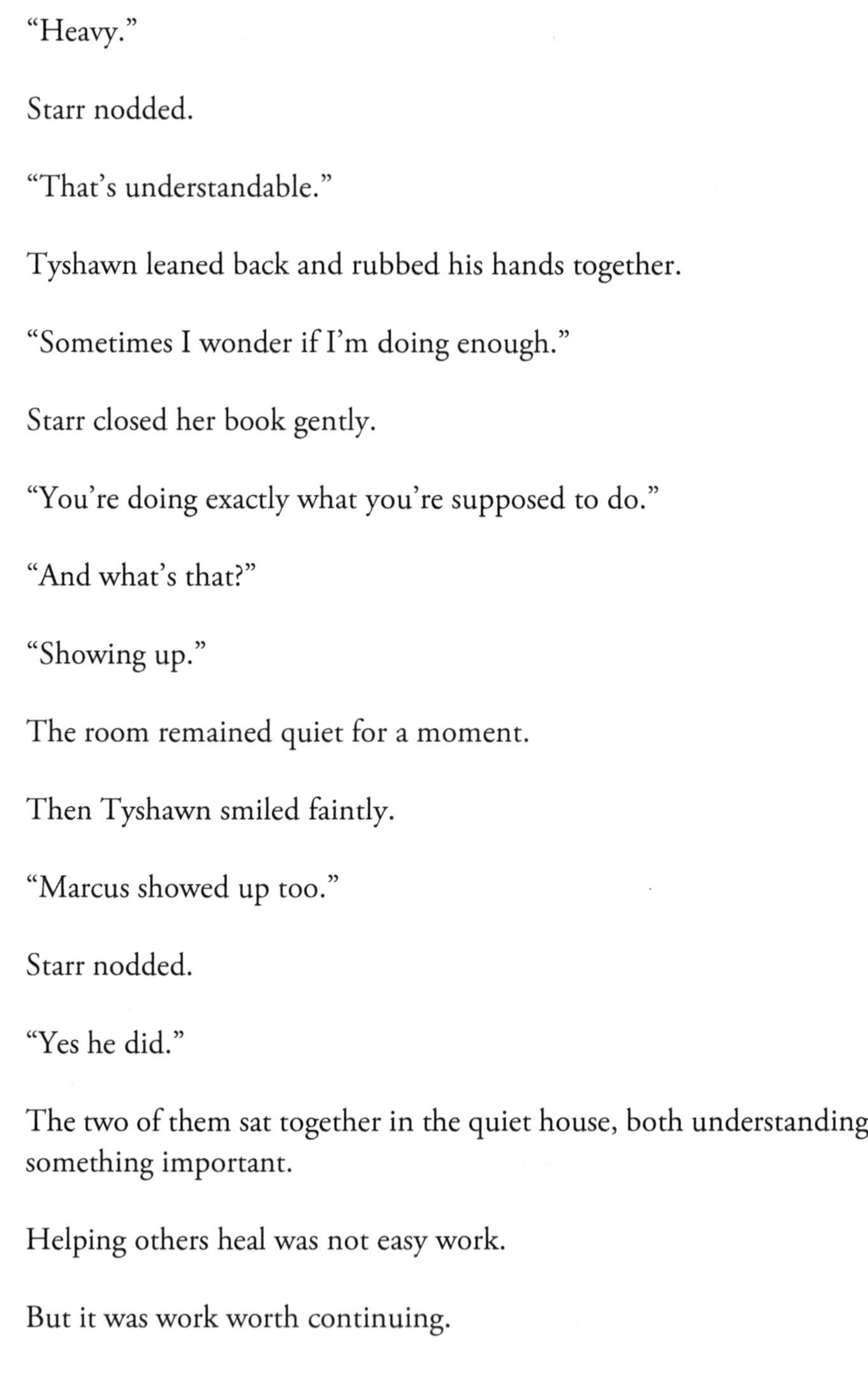

"Heavy."

Starr nodded.

"That's understandable."

Tyshawn leaned back and rubbed his hands together.

"Sometimes I wonder if I'm doing enough."

Starr closed her book gently.

"You're doing exactly what you're supposed to do."

"And what's that?"

"Showing up."

The room remained quiet for a moment.

Then Tyshawn smiled faintly.

"Marcus showed up too."

Starr nodded.

"Yes he did."

The two of them sat together in the quiet house, both understanding something important.

Helping others heal was not easy work.

But it was work worth continuing.

Even when the weight felt heavy.

CHAPTER 7

The Chair Breaks

Wednesday nights had become the busiest nights in the Carter household.

By the time the sun began setting, the house carried the sounds of preparation. The chairs were moved into place. The kettle warmed slowly on the stove. The living room was straightened and the hallway cleared so the children who often followed their mothers could sit comfortably together.

What started around the kitchen table had long outgrown that space.

Now the living room filled with women each week.

But even as the ministry grew, Starr kept the same quiet atmosphere she had from the beginning. There were no podiums. No microphones. No titles. Just chairs arranged in a circle and the understanding that this room was a place for honesty.

That evening the women arrived slowly.

Danielle came first.

She looked tired, but she still managed a small smile when Starr opened the door.

“Come on in,” Starr said gently.

Danielle stepped inside and sat in the same chair she often chose near the window.

Other women followed shortly after.

Some carried small dishes.

Others simply came with tired expressions and heavy hearts.

Once everyone settled into their seats, Starr began the conversation the same way she always did.

"How has everyone been this week?"

For a moment, no one spoke.

Finally, one woman sighed.

"My husband came home angry again."

Another woman nodded.

"Mine hasn't said two words all week."

Danielle looked down at her hands.

"He's not angry," she said quietly.

"He's just… lost."

The women looked at her carefully.

Starr spoke softly.

"Sometimes when men begin facing things they've buried for years, it can make them feel unstable for a while."

Danielle nodded.

"That's exactly how Marcus seems."

The room remained quiet as the conversation continued.

Some women shared stories of arguments at home.

Others spoke about confusion.

Several admitted they didn't know how to respond when their husbands suddenly became emotional.

Starr listened carefully.

Then she began explaining something she had seen many times in her work.

"When someone begins opening old wounds," she said calmly, "it can feel like their whole life is coming apart."

One woman frowned.

"Then why do it?"

"Because healing doesn't happen by ignoring pain," Starr replied.

"It happens by facing it."

The women nodded slowly.

But as the evening continued, the weight of the stories began settling into Starr's chest.

One woman described her husband's nightmares.

Another talked about childhood trauma her husband had finally admitted.

Another spoke about years of silence in her marriage.

The stories filled the room.

Pain.

Confusion.

Fear.

By the time the meeting ended, the women left quietly.

Several hugged Starr before stepping outside.

Danielle lingered last.

"Thank you," she said softly.

Starr smiled.

"You're doing better than you think."

After Danielle left, the house grew silent again.

The chairs remained arranged in the circle.

Tea cups sat half empty on the small tables.

Starr slowly began cleaning the room.

But as she stacked the last chair against the wall, something inside her shifted.

The weight of the evening settled over her all at once.

She walked slowly toward the chair by the window and sat down.

For several minutes she stared out at the quiet street.

The streetlight outside cast a soft glow across the pavement.

Inside the house, the silence felt heavy.

All the stories from the evening replayed in her mind.

The women who didn't understand how to help their husbands.

The men trying to face years of buried pain.

The marriages hang quietly between hope and exhaustion.

Starr closed her eyes.

For weeks she had carried these conversations calmly.

She had listened.

Guided.

Explained.

But tonight the weight felt heavier than usual.

Her shoulders began to shake slightly.

Tears slowly rolled down her face.

For the first time since the ministry began, Starr allowed herself to feel everything she had been holding inside.

She covered her face with her hands and quietly cried.

Upstairs, Jaunene sat on the steps outside her bedroom.

She had learned to recognize the sounds of the Wednesday meetings.

The voices.

The conversations.

The quiet moments when the women prayed together.

Tonight she heard something different.

She stood slowly and walked halfway down the stairs.

From there she could see the living room.

Her mother sat in the chair by the window with her head lowered.

Jaunene didn't move.

She simply watched it.

After a moment, the front door opened.

Tyshawn stepped inside.

He had just returned from the men's meeting at the church.

He removed his jacket and stopped when he saw Starr sitting by the window.

Even from across the room, he could see the tears on her face.

"Starr?"

She quickly wiped her eyes, but it was too late.

Tyshawn walked toward her slowly.

"What happened?"

Starr shook her head.

"Just a long night."

Tyshawn knelt beside the chair.

"You don't have to carry everything by yourself."

Starr let out a quiet breath.

"I know."

But the tears were returned.

Tyshawn sat beside her and gently took her hand.

For a moment neither of them spoke.

Then softly, almost instinctively, Tyshawn began singing.

"Never would have made it…"

His voice was low but steady.

"Never could have made it without You…"

Starr looked at him through her tears.

Tyshawn continued quietly.

"I would have lost it all…"

The words filled the room with something deeper than comfort.

Faith.

Starr leaned her head against his shoulder as the last words faded.

Across the room, Jaunene quietly stepped back up the stairs.

She returned to her bedroom without making a sound.

But the moment I stayed with her.

Downstairs, the house grew quiet again.

Starr sat in the chair by the window, her hand resting in Tyshawn's.

For the first time that night, the weight felt a little lighter.

Because sometimes the strongest people still need someone beside them.

And sometimes healing begins simply by allowing yourself to be seen.

CHAPTER 8

Healing in the House

The following Wednesday arrived quietly.

The house felt calm that afternoon, but Starr knew the evening would once again bring the familiar rhythm of voices, stories, and emotions that had begun filling the living room each week.

She moved slowly through the house preparing the space the same way she always did.

The chairs were arranged in a circle.

The kettle warmed on the stove.

A tray of tea cups rested on the coffee table.

There was something intentional about the way Starr prepared the room. She wanted the space to feel safe the moment someone walked through the door.

Safe enough for truth.

Safe enough for healing.

Jaunene sat at the kitchen table finishing her homework while watching her mother move quietly through the living room.

"You do the same thing every Wednesday," she said.

Starr smiled.

"Consistency helps people relax."

Jaunene nodded thoughtfully.

"Are the women sad again tonight?"

"Some of them will be."

"Why?"

Starr paused for a moment before answering.

"Because healing sometimes starts with talking about things that hurt."

Jaunene considered that.

Then she returned to her notebook.

Soon the doorbell rang.

Danielle stood outside again, this time carrying a small container of cookies.

"Thought we could use something sweet tonight," she said.

Starr welcomed her inside.

More women arrived shortly after.

Some brought tea.

One brought homemade bread.

Another carried a small dish of fruit.

What had started as simple conversations around a table now felt like a quiet gathering of support.

Once everyone was seated, Starr looked around the circle.

“How has everyone been since last week?”

One woman spoke first.

“My husband apologized for something he did ten years ago.”

Another woman nodded.

“Mine did too.”

The group laughed softly.

“It’s strange hearing apologies that late,” someone said.

“But it means something.”

Danielle sat quietly for a moment before speaking.

“Marcus has been different.”

The room grew still.

“He’s thinking a lot.”

"About what?" another woman asked.

"Everything."

Starr leaned forward slightly.

"That's actually a good sign."

Danielle looked surprised.

"It is?"

"Yes."

"When people begin facing things they've buried for years, it can make them quiet for a while."

Another woman sighed.

"My husband barely talks lately."

"That's part of the process," Starr explained.

"Men often process emotions internally before they know how to express them."

The women listened carefully.

Starr continued speaking gently but clearly.

"In counseling we sometimes describe this as emotional excavation."

Several women smiled at the unfamiliar phrase.

"What does that mean?" one asked.

"It means they're digging through old layers of their lives."

"Memories."

"Experiences."

"Pain."

"And sometimes when people dig that deeply, the ground becomes unstable before it becomes steady."

The women nodded slowly.

Danielle folded her hands together.

"I just want to help him."

"You are helping him," Starr said.

"How?"

"By being patient."

Another woman raised her hand slightly.

"But what if we don't know what to say?"

Starr smiled.

"You don't always need the perfect words."

"Then what do we do?"

“You listen.”

“Again with the listening,” one woman joked.

The room laughed.

But Starr nodded seriously.

“Yes.”

“Listening allows people to speak without fear.”

The conversation continued for nearly two hours.

Some women asked questions about trauma.

Others talked about arguments they had recently had with their husbands.

Several admitted they had never thought about how much pressure men carried silently.

Danielle eventually leaned back in her chair.

“I understand Marcus better now.”

Starr smiled.

“That’s the goal.”

Danielle nodded.

“I just wish he understood himself better.”

Starr's voice softened.

"He's trying."

The women sat quietly for a moment reflecting on that thought.

Upstairs Jaunene sat on the steps again.

She had grown used to listening quietly as the conversations drifted through the house.

Some of the words were difficult for her to understand.

But the tone was clear.

The women cared about one another.

They cared about their husbands.

And somehow, through those conversations, things were slowly getting better.

Back downstairs the meeting was coming to an end.

The women gathered their things.

Some hugged before leaving.

Others stood in small groups talking near the door.

Danielle lingered again.

"I feel lighter after these meetings," she admitted.

Starr nodded.

"That's what support does."

Danielle looked around the living room.

"It's amazing this all started at your kitchen table."

Starr smiled softly.

"Sometimes the smallest spaces hold the most important conversations."

After the women left, Starr once again sat in the chair by the window.

The street outside was quiet.

Tyshawn returned home shortly after the men's meeting at the church.

"How did it go tonight?" he asked.

Starr looked up.

"Better."

Tyshawn sat across from her.

"The men talked more tonight too."

Starr smiled.

"Maybe both groups are helping each other."

Tyshawn nodded thoughtfully.

Across the house Jaunene closed her notebook.

Without fully realizing it yet, she had begun learning something important.

Healing did not happen in one moment.

It happened slowly.

Through conversations.

Through patience.

Through people who were willing to sit together in the same room and tell the truth.

And inside that house on Wednesday nights, healing was quietly taking place.

CHAPTER 9

The Pastor Watching

Pastor Barrett had learned something important after decades of leading City Life Church.

Real ministry rarely announces itself.

It usually begins quietly.

A conversation in a hallway.

A prayer spoken between two people.

A small gathering that slowly becomes something larger than anyone expected.

That was why he had started paying closer attention to the things happening on Wednesday nights.

From his office window he often watched members of the church arrive long before Sunday services. Cars pulled into the parking lot in small groups. Some men walked inside the church building. Others gathered in the hallway speaking quietly before entering the classroom where Tyshawn hosted the empowerment meetings.

At first Pastor Barrett had simply been curious.

Now he was thoughtful.

One Wednesday evening he walked slowly down the hallway while the men's meeting had already begun. The classroom door was closed, but the voices inside carried through the thin walls.

He didn't interrupt.

Instead, he stood quietly for a moment listening.

Not to the details of the conversation.

But to the tone.

Men speaking honestly.

Sometimes laughing.

Sometimes it's quiet.

Sometimes it's emotional.

Pastor Barrett smiled to himself.

Years earlier he had prayed for the men in his congregation to become stronger spiritually and emotionally. But he had also understood something many churches struggled with.

Men rarely opened their hearts in large public spaces.

They opened them in smaller rooms.

Rooms where trust could grow.

He continued down the hallway and stepped into the sanctuary.

The large room sat empty except for the soft glow of the overhead lights. Pastor Barrett walked slowly to the front pew and sat down, resting his Bible beside him.

He thought about Tyshawn.

When Tyshawn first arrived at City Life Church years earlier, he had simply been a young funeral director trying to help grieving families navigate loss. Pastor Barrett had watched him closely even then.

Tyshawn listened differently than most people.

He didn't rush people through their pain.

He didn't speak simply to fill silence.

He listened.

That gift had slowly grown into something more.

Now men gathered weekly to talk about their lives.

And something else had begun growing alongside it.

The women's meetings at Starr's house.

Pastor Barrett had heard about them through quiet conversations with members of the church.

One Sunday morning a woman approached him after service.

"Pastor," she said, "I just want you to know something good is happening."

"What's that?"

"Starr has been helping the women understand what their husbands are going through."

Pastor Barrett nodded thoughtfully.

He had suspected as much.

Strong ministries often grew in pairs.

Support meeting support.

Healing meeting healing.

Later that evening he drove past the Carter home on his way back from visiting a church member.

Lights filled the living room window.

Several cars lined the street.

Pastor Barrett slowed the car slightly.

Through the window he could see the circle of women sitting together.

Listening.

Talking.

Supporting one another.

He continued driving but the image stayed in his mind.

When he arrived home he sat quietly in his study for a while.

His Bible rested open on the desk.

He thought about the future of the church.

Leadership was not only about guiding people in the present.

It was also about preparing the church for the years ahead.

And Pastor Barrett knew something many others had not yet realized.

City Life Church was changing.

Not in structure.

But in spirit.

The conversations happening in those small groups were transforming families.

Men were becoming more honest.

Women were becoming more understanding.

Marriages were healing.

Children were watching their parents grow.

A quiet smile crossed his face.

He had spent decades preaching sermons from the pulpit.

But sometimes the most powerful work of the church happened far away from the pulpit.

It happened in living rooms.

Around kitchen tables.

Inside circles of chairs where people finally felt safe enough to speak the truth.

The following Sunday morning, the sanctuary filled with members as usual.

Pastor Barrett stood behind the pulpit and looked across the congregation.

His eyes paused briefly on Tyshawn sitting with several of the men from the empowerment group.

Then his eyes moved toward Starr sitting beside Jaunene.

The two ministries were growing quietly side by side.

And Pastor Barrett understood something important.

God had already begun raising the next generation of leadership within the church.

The congregation waited as he prepared to speak.

Pastor Barrett rested his hands on the pulpit and smiled gently.

"Sometimes," he began, "the greatest work God does in a church happens when people begin caring for one another in ways we never planned."

Several members nodded.

"Ministry isn't always about programs."

"It's about people."

He glanced again toward Tyshawn and Starr.

"And sometimes the most powerful ministry begins when someone simply opens their door… and listens."

The congregation remained quiet as the meaning of his words settled into their hearts.

Pastor Barrett closed his Bible slowly.

The church was growing.

Not because of the strategy.

But because healing had found a home among its people.

And as he stood there behind the pulpit, Pastor Barrett understood something clearly.

The future of City Life Church was already unfolding before his eyes.

CHAPTER 10

The Church Growing

City Life Church began changing in ways that were impossible to ignore.

At first the difference was subtle.

A few more cars appeared in the parking lot on Wednesday evenings. Members who normally came only on Sundays started arriving in the middle of the week. Conversations lingered longer in the hallways after service.

But within a few months the shift became obvious.

The empowerment group that once fit comfortably inside a small classroom now filled nearly every chair in the room. Some men leaned against the walls. Others stood quietly in the back listening.

Tyshawn noticed it the moment he walked in one Wednesday evening.

James looked around and laughed.

"We might need a bigger room."

Tyshawn smiled.

"That's a good problem to have."

Several of the men greeted new faces that night. Word had spread quietly throughout the community. Men who had heard about the conversations happening at City Life Church began showing up.

Some came because a friend invited them.

Some came because their wives encouraged them.

Some came simply because they were tired of carrying things alone.

Tyshawn welcomed each of them the same way.

“Grab a chair,” he would say.

“If there’s not one, we’ll make space.”

Across town, the women’s gathering had also begun growing.

What once fit easily around Starr’s kitchen table had moved fully into the living room. Even that space was beginning to feel crowded.

One Wednesday evening, as the women settled into their chairs, Danielle looked around the room and smiled.

“We’ve doubled since last month.”

Starr nodded thoughtfully.

“People are inviting their friends.”

“That’s usually how healing spreads,” Danielle said.

“Through trust.”

The conversations that night moved deeper than usual.

One woman spoke about years of misunderstanding in her marriage.

Another admitted she had never realized how much pressure her husband carried until he began attending the men's meetings.

Starr listened carefully.

Then she spoke gently.

"When one person in a family begins healing, it affects everyone around them."

The women nodded slowly.

"That's why what's happening here matters," she continued.

"It's not just helping the men."

"It's helping entire families."

Upstairs, Jaunene sat on the steps again with her notebook resting on her knees.

She had begun writing down words she heard during the meetings.

Not full sentences.

Just thoughts.

"Listening helps."

"Healing takes time."

"People carry things they never say."

She didn't fully understand everything yet.

But she knew the conversations were important.

Back at the church the men's meeting was in full conversation.

One of the new members spoke nervously.

"I almost didn't come tonight."

Tyshawn leaned forward slightly.

"What made you change your mind?"

"My wife."

The room laughed softly.

"She told me I've been angry for years and don't even know why."

Another man nodded.

"That sounds familiar."

The group laughed again, but the laughter carried understanding rather than judgment.

Tyshawn spoke calmly.

"Anger is often the emotion people see first."

"What's underneath it?" one man asked.

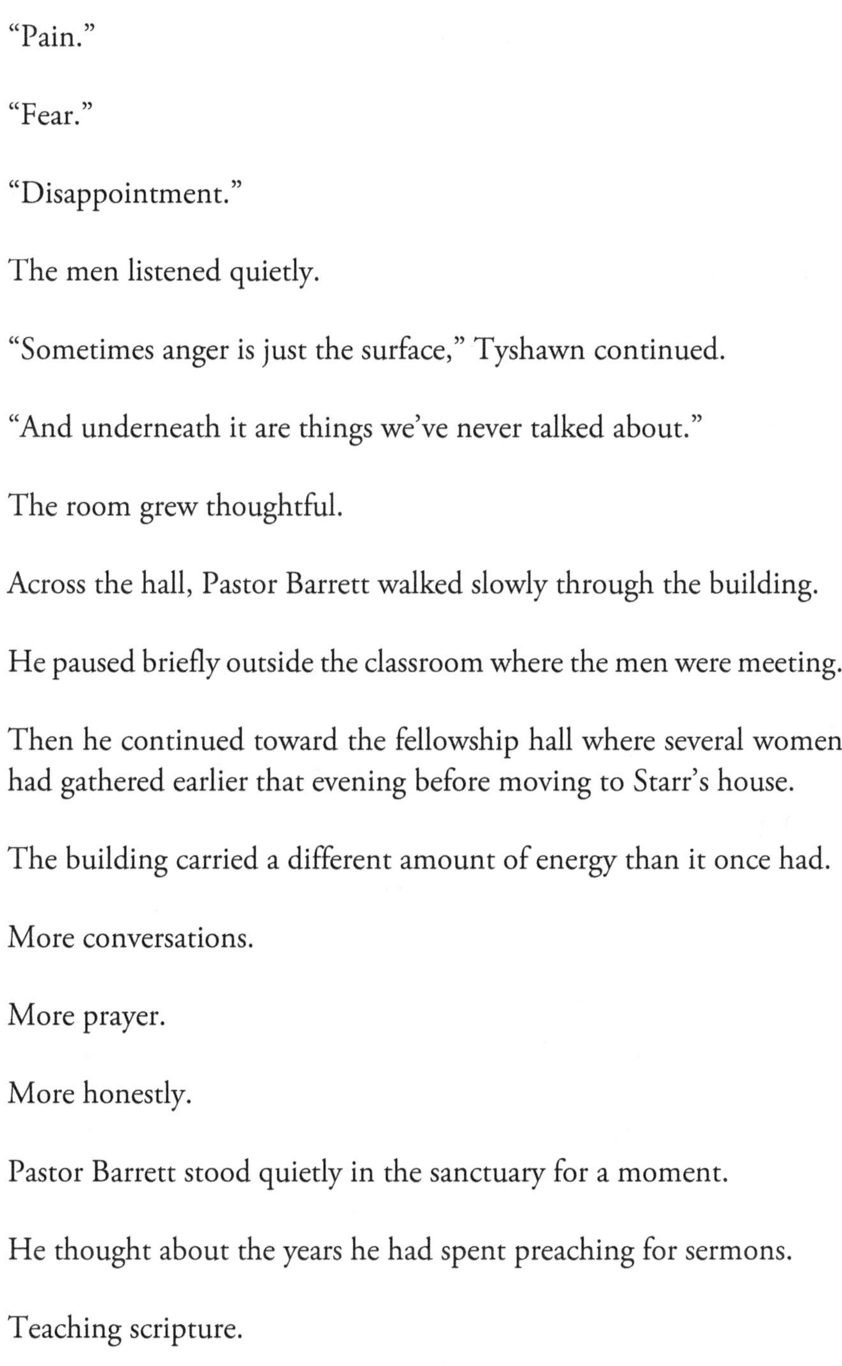

"Pain."

"Fear."

"Disappointment."

The men listened quietly.

"Sometimes anger is just the surface," Tyshawn continued.

"And underneath it are things we've never talked about."

The room grew thoughtful.

Across the hall, Pastor Barrett walked slowly through the building.

He paused briefly outside the classroom where the men were meeting.

Then he continued toward the fellowship hall where several women had gathered earlier that evening before moving to Starr's house.

The building carried a different amount of energy than it once had.

More conversations.

More prayer.

More honestly.

Pastor Barrett stood quietly in the sanctuary for a moment.

He thought about the years he had spent preaching for sermons.

Teaching scripture.

Leading the church through its seasons.

But what he saw happening now felt different.

The church was no longer just a place where people came to worship.

It had become a place where people came to heal.

And the healing was spreading beyond the church walls.

Marriages were changing.

Families were changing.

Even the children were beginning to notice.

Later that evening, Tyshawn returned home after the men's meeting.

The house was quiet except for the faint sound of conversation still drifting from the living room where the last few women remained with Starr.

Tyshawn walked into the kitchen and poured himself a glass of water.

Jaunene sat at the table drawing in her notebook.

"What are you working on?" he asked.

"Just writing things down."

"Like what?"

"Things people say."

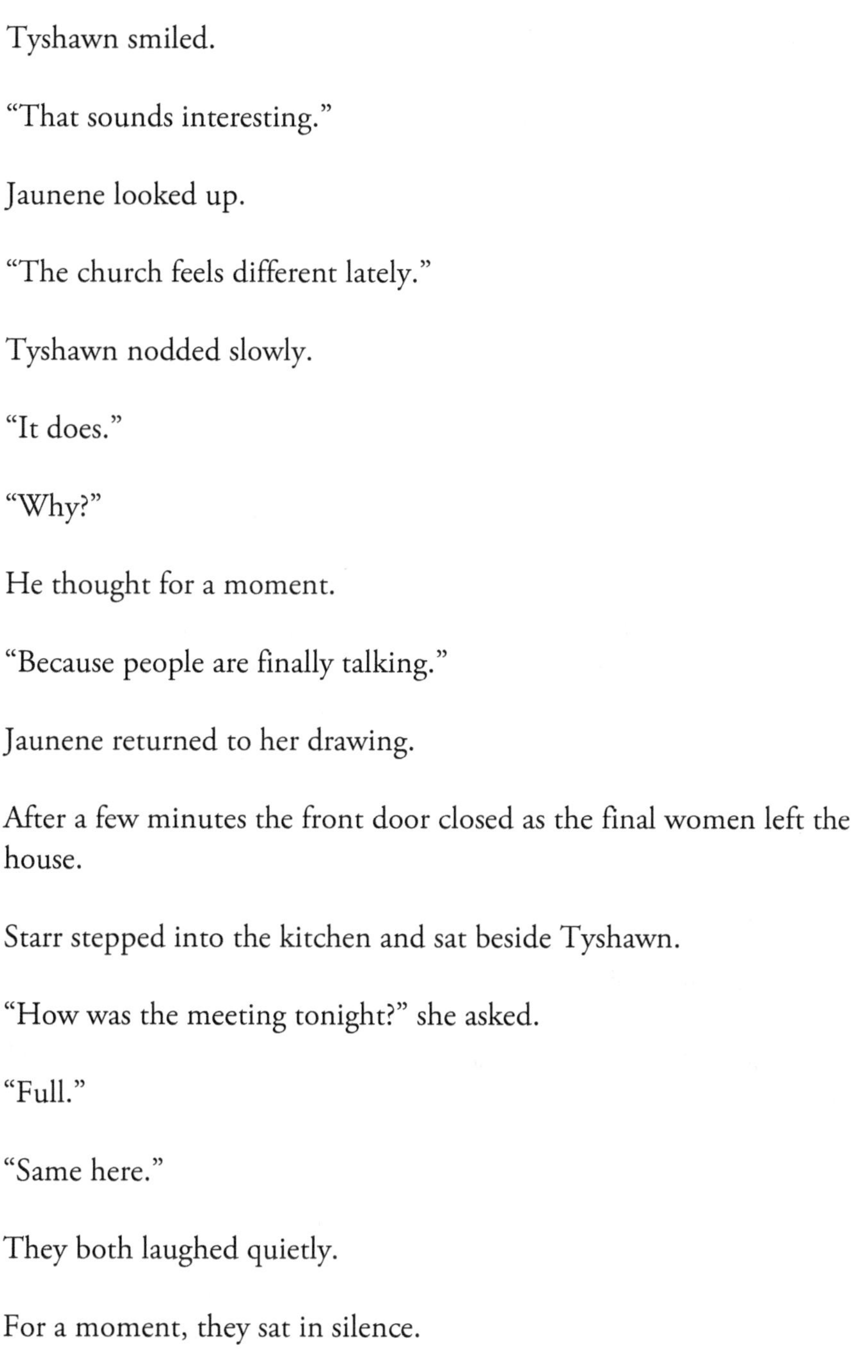

Tyshawn smiled.

“That sounds interesting.”

Jaunene looked up.

“The church feels different lately.”

Tyshawn nodded slowly.

“It does.”

“Why?”

He thought for a moment.

“Because people are finally talking.”

Jaunene returned to her drawing.

After a few minutes the front door closed as the final women left the house.

Starr stepped into the kitchen and sat beside Tyshawn.

“How was the meeting tonight?” she asked.

“Full.”

“Same here.”

They both laughed quietly.

For a moment, they sat in silence.

Then Starr looked toward the living room.

"Maybe we should start meeting at the church soon."

Tyshawn nodded.

"It might be time."

Across the house, Jaunene listened quietly.

Without realizing it, she was watching something important unfold.

The ministries that began with simple conversations were now filling rooms.

And the church that once held quiet Sunday services had become a place where people came searching for something deeper.

Hope.

Understanding.

Healing.

City Life Church was growing.

And none of them fully understood yet just how far that growth would reach.

CHAPTER 11

Starr Knows

Wednesday nights had become the heartbeat of City Life Church.

By the time the sun set, the parking lot would already begin filling with cars. Men walked through the front entrance greeting one another with handshakes and quiet laughter. Women gathered in the fellowship hall or sometimes at Starr's house depending on the week. Children ran down the hallway until Jaunene gently reminded them to lower their voices.

Healing had found a home there.

What began as a small circle around a kitchen table had now grown into two full ministries that the church embraced with open arms.

That night felt no different at first.

The men filled the meeting room with the familiar sound of chairs sliding into a circle. Tyshawn moved calmly through the space greeting each man the way he always did. He was never the loudest voice in the room, but his presence carried a steady calm that people trusted.

Across the building, Starr arranged the chairs in the fellowship room.

The tea kettle steamed quietly on a nearby table. Several women helped place small trays of food and cups along the counter. The room carried the gentle warmth of women preparing a safe place for honest conversation.

Starr looked toward the door as the last woman entered.

“Everyone comfortable?” she asked.

Several heads nodded.

“Good,” Starr said softly. “Let’s begin.”

The conversations that followed moved slowly, carefully.

One woman spoke about how difficult it had been hearing her husband describe childhood abuse for the first time. Another talked about how the men’s group had opened conversations at home that had never happened before.

Starr listened.

That was always her greatest gift.

Listening.

She did not rush people.

She did not force advice.

She simply allowed truth to breathe inside the room.

“Understanding someone’s pain,” she explained gently, “doesn’t mean you carry it for them.”

The women leaned forward.

"It means you walk beside them while they carry it themselves."

Several women nodded quietly.

From down the hallway came the faint sound of the men's voices rising and falling as Tyshawn guided their own discussion.

The church felt alive.

When the meeting finally ended, the women slowly gathered their things.

Hugs were exchanged.

Encouraging words whispered.

One by one they left the building.

Starr remained behind, stacking the last of the chairs.

The hallway had grown quiet.

Only a few lights remained on in the sanctuary.

As she walked toward the front of the church, she noticed someone sitting alone in one of the front pews.

Pastor Barrett.

He leaned slightly forward, his elbows resting on his knees as if catching his breath.

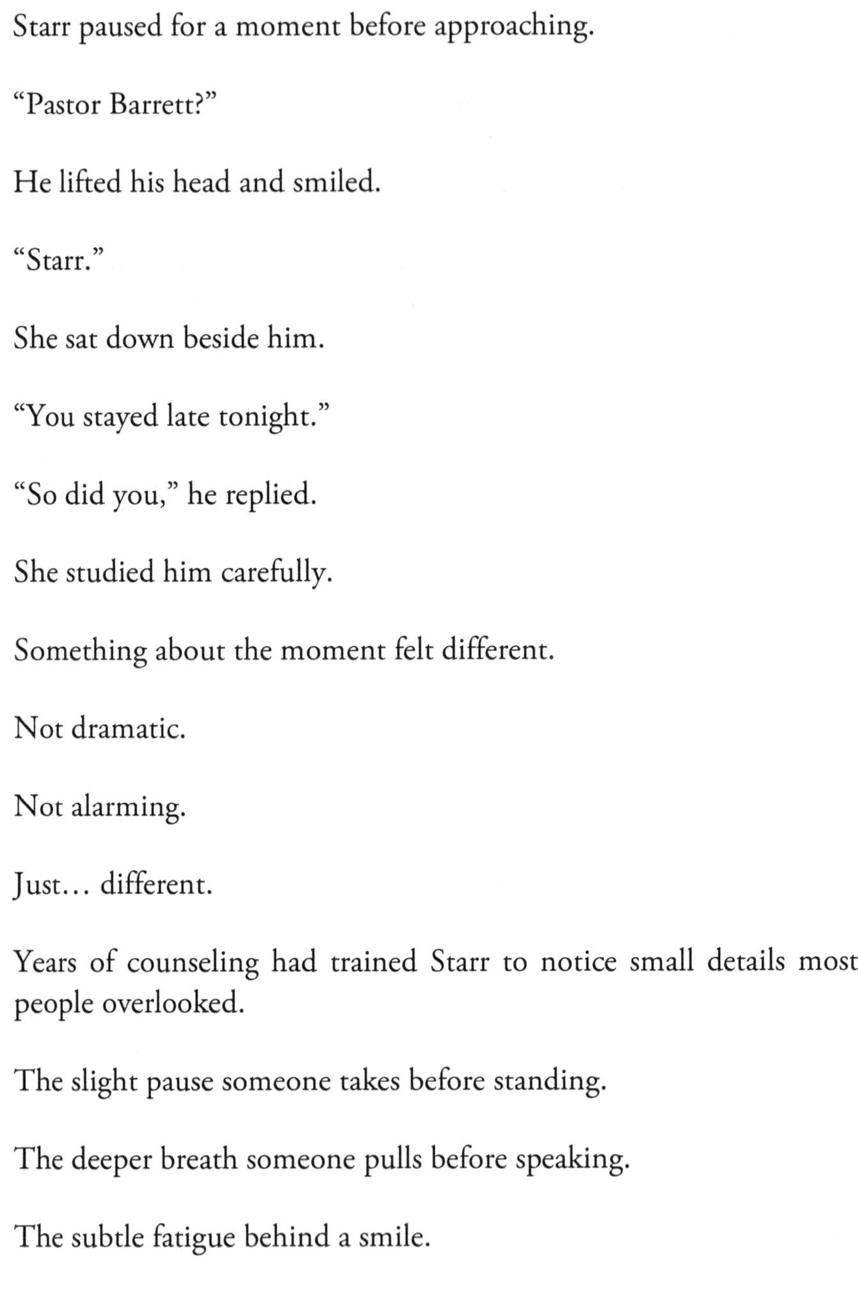

Starr paused for a moment before approaching.

"Pastor Barrett?"

He lifted his head and smiled.

"Starr."

She sat down beside him.

"You stayed late tonight."

"So did you," he replied.

She studied him carefully.

Something about the moment felt different.

Not dramatic.

Not alarming.

Just… different.

Years of counseling had trained Starr to notice small details most people overlooked.

The slight pause someone takes before standing.

The deeper breath someone pulls before speaking.

The subtle fatigue behind a smile.

She had seen those signs many times before when people tried to hide how tired they truly were.

“Are you alright?” she asked gently.

Pastor Barrett leaned back against the pew.

“I’ve been running this church for a long time,” he said with a soft chuckle.

“That’s not what I asked.”

He smiled again.

“You always listen carefully.”

The sanctuary was quiet except for the faint hum of the lights overhead.

Pastor Barrett reached into the pocket of his jacket and removed his Bible.

His fingers turned slowly through the pages until he stopped.

He handed the book to Starr.

“Read this.”

She glanced down and read aloud.

“To everything there is a season, and a time to every purpose under the heaven.”

Her eyes moved to the next verse.

"A time to keep silence, and a time to speak."

Ecclesiastes.

Starr closed the Bible slowly.

Pastor Barrett looked across the empty sanctuary.

"Tyshawn carries a lot right now," he said quietly.

The funeral home.

His doctoral studies.

The men who leaned on him every week.

The church itself.

"He has a good heart," the pastor continued. "But sometimes when a man is carrying too much weight, the best thing we can do is help him keep walking forward."

Starr listened carefully.

He had not asked her to hide anything.

He had simply spoken about wisdom.

About timing.

"There will come a moment when every conversation needs to happen," Pastor Barrett said gently.

"But wisdom helps us recognize when that moment arrives."

He stood slowly from the pew.

Starr noticed again the slight hesitation in his movement.

Small.

But real.

Pastor Barrett rested a hand briefly on the back of the pew before straightening fully.

"You've been a steady voice for many people," he said kindly.

"Keep helping Tyshawn stay focused on the path God is setting before him."

Starr nodded quietly.

"I will."

Pastor Barrett smiled and began walking slowly toward the hallway.

Starr remained seated for several minutes after he left.

The sanctuary felt peaceful.

But her mind continued replaying the small details she had noticed.

The controlled breathing.

The careful movements.

The quiet fatigue behind his smile.

A season was changing.

Later that night, Starr sat in the chair by the window at home.

The street outside was calm beneath the glow of the streetlight.

The Bible rested in her lap.

She opened again to Ecclesiastes.

"A time to keep silence, and a time to speak."

Starr closed the book gently and looked toward the hallway where Tyshawn's office light still glowed beneath the door.

He was studying again.

Preparing for the future.

For now, her role was clear.

She would keep him steady.

She would keep him focused.

And when the time came to speak, he would be ready.

CHAPTER 12

The Announcement

Sunday morning arrived with a quiet anticipation that seemed to rest over City Life Church before the doors even opened.

The sun rose slowly through a thin layer of clouds, casting soft light across the church parking lot as the first cars began to arrive. Families stepped out greeting one another with warm smiles and familiar handshakes. Children hurried toward the entrance while parents followed close behind, reminding them to slow down before reaching the doors.

Inside the building, the ushers were already preparing the sanctuary.

Programs were placed neatly on the ends of the pews. The choir gathered near the front reviewing the morning hymn. The sound of quiet conversation filled the room as people settled into their seats.

Something about the morning felt different.

No one could quite explain it.

But people sensed it.

Tyshawn entered through the side hallway with a few of the men from the empowerment group walking beside him. Their conversations were light but thoughtful, the kind that often followed long weeks of honest discussions inside the group.

James glanced around the sanctuary.

“Looks like a full house today,” he said quietly.

Tyshawn followed his gaze.

More people were arriving than usual.

Members who sometimes attended only once or twice a month had returned that morning. Several unfamiliar faces sat toward the back rows. A few people Tyshawn recognized from the university stood near the entrance greeting church members politely.

One of them waved when he saw him.

“Tyshawn!”

Tyshawn smiled and walked over.

“You made it.”

“We’ve been hearing about this place all semester,” one of the students said. “Figured we should finally see what all the talk was about.”

Tyshawn laughed softly.

“Well, welcome.”

Another student nodded toward the front of the church.

“This is the church where the empowerment group meets?”

“That’s right,” Tyshawn replied.

“We’ve heard a lot about what’s happening here,” another classmate added. “A church where people actually talk about real struggles.”

Tyshawn shrugged humbly.

“People just needed a place where they could be honest.”

Across the sanctuary Starr sat beside Jaunene near the front pew.

Jaunene looked at the room carefully.

She had always been observant, noticing small details others overlooked.

The way the choir director whispered something to one of the elders.

The way several members of the church leadership sat together near the front row.

The way Pastor Barrett moved slightly slower as he walked toward the pulpit.

Starr noticed it too.

The congregation stood as the service began.

The choir lifted their voices in a familiar hymn that filled the sanctuary with warmth. The music settled over the room gently, calming the quiet anticipation that seemed to rest among the congregation.

When the hymn ended, Pastor Barrett stepped forward.

He placed both hands on the pulpit and looked out across the sanctuary.

For a moment, he simply observed the people before him.

The families who had worshiped there for decades.

The new members who had joined in recent months.

The men whose lives had changed through the empowerment group.

The women who gathered each week with Starr to strengthen their marriages and support one another.

The church had grown.

But more importantly, it had healed.

Pastor Barrett smiled softly.

"I have an announcement to make this morning."

The room grew still.

"Over the past several years many of you have witnessed something happening in this church."

He paused.

"You have seen a ministry grow quietly among us."

Several members nodded.

"You have watched families begin healing."

He looked toward the section where the men from the empowerment group sat together.

"You have watched husbands find the courage to tell the truth about their lives."

Then he turned toward the women seated nearby.

"And you have watched wives learn how to walk beside them through that healing."

His eyes slowly moved across the congregation until they rested on Tyshawn.

"And at the center of much of that work has been a man many of you already know."

Tyshawn shifted slightly in his seat.

Pastor Barrett continued.

"Tyshawn has served this community faithfully as a funeral director."

Heads nodded throughout the sanctuary.

"He has stood beside families during their most painful moments."

"He has comforted those who believed their grief would never ease."

"He has helped men discover that strength often begins with honesty."

The congregation listened quietly.

“In addition to his work with families, Tyshawn has spent the past several years studying the human mind, grief, and the process of healing.”

Several of Tyshawn’s classmates smiled from the back rows.

“Through those studies, and through his service to this church, it has become clear that God has placed a calling on his life.”

The elders stood quietly behind the pulpit.

“For that reason,” Pastor Barrett said, “next Sunday evening we will gather here in this sanctuary to formally ordain Tyshawn into ministry.”

A gentle murmur moved through the congregation.

Many people smiled.

The men from the empowerment group exchanged proud looks with one another.

Across the sanctuary, Tyshawn sat very still.

He had not expected this.

Pastor Barrett lifted his hand slightly.

“Ordination does not create a minister.”

The sanctuary quieted again.

“It simply recognizes the ministry God has already been doing in someone’s life.”

The congregation responded with soft applause.

Starr reached over and gently squeezed Tyshawn's hand.

Jaunene leaned toward him.

"Is something big happening next week?" she whispered.

Tyshawn smiled slightly.

"I think it is."

Pastor Barrett concluded the announcement with a quiet reflection.

"This church has always believed that healing happens when people walk through life together."

He looked across the congregation one more time.

"Next Sunday we will celebrate the work that God has already begun among us."

The choir rose again to sing.

But the atmosphere inside the sanctuary had shifted.

People understood they were preparing something meaningful.

Across the room Starr watched Pastor Barrett carefully as he stepped away from the pulpit.

Again, she noticed the small details.

The careful pace of his steps.

The brief pause before he sat down.

The quiet fatigue behind his gentle smile.

The scripture from Ecclesiastes returned to her mind.

A time to keep silent.

A time to speak.

For now, she would remain quiet.

She glanced toward Tyshawn, sitting beside her.

He was still processing what had just been announced.

Starr gently placed her hand on his.

“Looks like next Sunday will be important,” she said softly.

Tyshawn nodded slowly.

“Yes.”

Neither of them realized yet just how important that moment would become.

CHAPTER 13

The Night Before Ordination

The week between the announcement and the ordination moved faster than Tyshawn expected.

At first, he tried to continue his routine the way he always had.

Funeral home meetings still need to be handled. Families still called in the middle of the night needing guidance. The empowerment group still gathered on Wednesday evenings with the same honesty and vulnerability that had become the heart of the ministry.

But beneath all of that normal rhythm, something had changed.

Everywhere Tyshawn went that week, people stopped him.

Church members shook his hand.

Men from the empowerment group embraced him.

Women from Starr's ministry smiled with quiet pride.

"Pastor Barrett made a good decision," one man said.

Tyshawn always gave the same humble response.

"I'm still just Tyshawn."

But inside, he understood the weight of what was coming.

Ordination was not about a title.

It was about responsibility.

Late Saturday afternoon, the church parking lot slowly began filling again.

Cars from neighboring towns pulled into spaces. A small church van arrived carrying a group of pastors who had traveled together to attend the ceremony the next evening.

Inside the church building, volunteers moved through the sanctuary preparing everything for the service.

Fresh flowers were arranged near the pulpit.

Extra chairs were placed along the back wall.

The choir rehearsed quietly near the stage.

Starr walked slowly down the center aisle, reviewing the final preparations.

She checked the arrangement table.

She spoke briefly with the ushers.

She thanked the women who had helped prepare refreshments for the fellowship gathering that would follow the ceremony.

Starr had always been good at organizing quiet details.

Tyshawn noticed that about her long ago.

Where he carried the emotional weight of people's stories, Starr carried the structure that kept everything steady.

Jaunene followed her mother through the sanctuary holding a small notebook.

She watched everything carefully.

"Why are so many people coming tomorrow?" She asked.

Starr smiled gently.

"Because something important is happening."

Jaunene nodded thoughtfully.

Across the building, Tyshawn stood near the front doors greeting several of his classmates as they arrived.

One of them shook his head in amazement as he stepped inside.

"You didn't tell us this church was this beautiful."

Tyshawn laughed softly.

"It's not about the building."

"No," the student replied, looking around the sanctuary. "It's about what's happening here."

Another classmate nodded.

"In our counseling classes we talk about grief theory all the time. But watching what you've been doing here… that's real life."

Tyshawn shrugged slightly.

"People just needed a place to speak honestly."

"You built that place," the classmate said.

Tyshawn shook his head.

"God built it."

As the evening moved on, the sanctuary slowly emptied again.

The pastors who had traveled into town left for their hotels.

The volunteers finished the last of their preparations.

Soon only a few lights remained inside the building.

Tyshawn and Starr stayed behind for a few quiet minutes before leaving.

They sat together in the front pew.

The sanctuary felt peaceful.

Tyshawn leaned back slightly.

"I never expected any of this."

Starr turned toward him.

“What part?”

“All of it.”

He gestured toward the room.

“The empowerment group. The church. The ordination tomorrow.”

He shook his head slowly.

“I was just trying to help a few men talk honestly.”

Starr smiled softly.

“That’s usually how real ministry begins.”

Tyshawn looked down at his hands.

“Sometimes I still feel like I’m not ready.”

Starr reached over and gently placed her hand on his.

“You’ve been doing the work for years.”

He looked at her.

“The ceremony tomorrow just recognizes what’s already been happening.”

From the back of the sanctuary, Pastor Barrett quietly watched them.

He had entered through the side door without disturbing the moment.

The sight before him brought a peaceful smile to his face.

Tyshawn is sitting in a quiet reflection.

Starr beside him, offering calm wisdom.

Jaunene sitting a few rows behind them drawing pictures quietly in her notebook.

The future of the church was already forming before his eyes.

He stepped forward slowly.

Tyshawn looked up when he heard the footsteps.

"Pastor Barrett."

The older man smiled warmly.

"Just checking on the final preparations."

Tyshawn stood.

"Everything should be ready for tomorrow."

Pastor Barrett nodded.

"I believe it will be."

He glanced around the sanctuary.

Then he looked back at Tyshawn.

"Get some rest tonight."

Tyshawn laughed lightly.

"I'll try."

The pastor rested a hand briefly on his shoulder.

"Tomorrow is an important day."

Tyshawn nodded.

"Yes, it is."

But as Pastor Barrett turned toward the hallway, Starr noticed something again.

A small hesitation in his step.

The careful way he steadied himself for just a moment before continuing forward.

No one else seemed to notice.

But Starr did.

She watched quietly as he disappeared down the hallway.

Then she turned back toward Tyshawn.

"Come on," she said gently.

"We should go home."

Tyshawn stood and looked around the sanctuary one last time before leaving.

The room was quiet again.

The flowers waited near the pulpit.

The chairs stood ready.

The church was prepared.

Tomorrow would be a day the congregation would never forget.

CHAPTER 14

The Ordination Ceremony

Sunday evening arrived with a quiet sense of reverence that seemed to settle over City Life Church long before the service began.

By late afternoon the parking lot was already filling with cars. Families arrived dressed in their Sunday best, greeting one another with warm smiles and quiet excitement. Word had spread quickly throughout the community during the week.

Tyshawn's ordination was not just another church event.

It was something the congregation felt connected to personally.

Inside the sanctuary, ushers guided people to their seats as more visitors entered the building. Several pastors from neighboring churches had arrived to support the service. Tyshawn's classmates from the university sat together along one side of the sanctuary, speaking quietly among themselves while observing the church that had become such an important part of his story.

The choir stood near the front preparing for the opening hymn.

Fresh flowers rested beside the pulpit.

Extra chairs lined up the back wall for guests.

By the time the service began, the sanctuary was full.

Starr sat near the front beside Jaunene.

Jaunene's eyes moved carefully across the room, absorbing every detail.

"This is bigger than Wednesday night," she whispered.

Starr smiled softly.

"Yes, it is."

Across the aisle the men from the empowerment group sat together. Many of them dressed carefully for the occasion, their posture carrying quiet pride as they waited for the service to begin.

Tyshawn stood near the front of the sanctuary speaking briefly with one of the visiting pastors.

He looked calm outside.

But inside his thoughts moved quickly.

He had directed hundreds of funerals.

He had counseled grieving families.

He had helped men speak openly about their lives for the first time.

Yet standing in front of his own church for this moment felt different.

This was not about helping someone else.

This was about accepting responsibility for the ministry that had grown around him.

The choir rose and the service began.

The opening hymn filled the sanctuary with a warm harmony that settled the room into quiet reflection.

When the song ended, Pastor Barrett stepped slowly toward the pulpit.

The congregation stood as he opened the service in prayer.

“Lord,” he said gently, “we thank You for gathering us together tonight.”

“We thank You for the work You have already been doing among us.”

“And we thank You for the people You call to serve Your children with compassion and humility.”

The congregation responded softly.

“Amen.”

After the prayer, a visiting minister stepped forward to deliver the charge.

He was a respected pastor from a neighboring church who had known Pastor Barrett for many years.

His voice carried a steady warmth as he spoke.

"Ordination is not about elevating a man," he began.

"It is about recognizing the work God has already placed in his life."

He looked toward Tyshawn.

"Ministry is not measured by the number of sermons preached."

"It is measured by the number of lives touched."

The sanctuary remained silent as he continued.

"A true minister walks beside people during their darkest moments."

"He listens when others are silent."

"He offers hope when someone believes hope has disappeared."

Several of the men from the empowerment group nodded quietly.

The visiting pastor finished with a final reflection.

"Tonight we recognize a man who has already been doing the work of ministry."

He stepped back from the pulpit.

Pastor Barrett returned to the front.

He looked toward Tyshawn.

"Tyshawn," he said gently.

"Come forward."

Tyshawn walked slowly to the front of the sanctuary.

For a moment he stood facing the congregation.

The room was completely still.

Pastor Barrett spoke clearly.

"Tyshawn has served this community faithfully for many years."

"He has comforted grieving families through his work at the funeral home."

"He has helped men find honesty through the empowerment group."

"And through his studies in psychology and grief counseling, he has committed himself to understanding the deeper work of healing."

He paused.

"Ordination does not create this calling."

"It simply recognizes what God has already been doing."

The elders of the church stood and gathered around Tyshawn.

Pastor Barrett looked at him kindly.

"Do you accept the calling to serve God's people with compassion, humility, and truth?"

Tyshawn took a slow breath.

"Yes," he answered.

The elders placed their hands gently on his shoulders.

The congregation bowed their heads.

Pastor Barrett prayed softly.

“Lord, we thank You for the work You have already begun in this man’s life.”

“Give him wisdom as he counsels those who grieve.”

“Give him strength when the weight of other people’s pain becomes heavy.”

“And remind him that true ministry is always rooted in love.”

The prayer ended in quiet reverence.

Pastor Barrett then reached for the Bible he had carried with him for many years.

The leather cover showed the gentle wear of time and countless sermons.

He placed the Bible in Tyshawn’s hands.

“This Bible has walked with me through many seasons,” he said softly.

“Tonight I pass it to you.”

The congregation watched silently.

“May it guide your words.”

"May it steady your heart."

"And may it remind you that every person you serve carries a story worth listening to."

He stepped back.

"By the authority given to the church, we now recognize Tyshawn as an ordained minister of the Gospel."

For a moment the room remained quiet.

Then the congregation rose to their feet.

Applause filled the sanctuary.

Several of Tyshawn's classmates stood as well, moved by the ceremony they had just witnessed.

The men from the empowerment group embraced one another proudly.

Starr wiped a quiet tear from her eye.

Jaunene looked up at her father.

"Does this mean everything will change now?" she asked softly.

Tyshawn smiled gently.

"No."

"What changes then?"

He thought for a moment.

"Now I just keep helping people heal."

From the side of the sanctuary, Pastor Barrett watched the moment quietly.

The church had just witnessed something sacred.

The future of the ministry had been placed into capable hands.

And though few people realized it yet, the passing of that Bible had marked the beginning of a new chapter for City Life Church.

CHAPTER 15

The Pastor's Quiet Decline

In the weeks that followed the ordination, life at City Life Church continued with the same steady rhythm that had grown over the past year.

Sunday services filled the sanctuary with familiar hymns and warm greetings. Wednesday evenings remained the heart of the ministries that had changed so many lives. The men's empowerment group continued meeting in the church classrooms while the women gathered faithfully around Starr's leadership.

To most of the congregation, everything appeared normal.

But Starr noticed the small changes.

They were subtle at first.

Pastor Barrett still preached every Sunday, his voice steady and thoughtful as always. His sermons carried the same wisdom the church had trusted for decades. But after each message he seemed to linger a little longer at the pulpit before stepping away.

Sometimes he rested his hand briefly against the side of the podium.

Sometimes he paused quietly before walking down the steps.

Most people didn't notice.

But Starr did.

Years of counseling had taught her to read the small signs that revealed when someone was carrying more than they allowed others to see.

One Wednesday evening she stood in the hallway outside the sanctuary while the men gathered for their meeting.

Tyshawn's voice drifted from the room as he welcomed the group.

The men laughed lightly as they settled into their chairs.

Across the building, the women had already begun their own meeting.

The church felt alive with conversation and prayer.

Pastor Barrett walked slowly down the hallway.

When he saw Starr he smiled warmly.

"Looks like another full house tonight."

She nodded.

"The ministries are growing faster than we expected."

"That's what happens when people finally feel safe enough to tell the truth," he replied.

Starr studied him for a moment.

"You should sit down for a few minutes before the service," she said gently.

He chuckled.

"You sound like a doctor."

"Just observant."

Pastor Barrett leaned lightly against the wall for a moment before continuing down the hallway.

"I've been running this church a long time," he said.

"That usually means someone else will be running it someday."

Starr understood what he meant.

But she also understood something he didn't say.

Time was moving forward.

Later that night, after both meetings ended, the church slowly emptied.

The last of the members left through the front doors while the custodians turned off the hallway lights.

Tyshawn stayed behind speaking with several of the men who needed a few extra minutes to talk.

Starr finished gathering the teacups from the women's meeting.

When she stepped into the sanctuary, she saw Pastor Barrett sitting quietly in the front pew.

His Bible rested beside him.

He looked peaceful.

For a moment she simply watched him.

"You're still here," she said softly.

He smiled.

"This room has always helped me think."

She sat beside him.

The sanctuary lights cast a soft glow across the empty pews.

"You've built something special here," Starr said.

Pastor Barrett shook his head gently.

"God builds the church."

"We just take care of the people."

He glanced toward the back of the sanctuary where Tyshawn's voice could still be heard faintly through the hallway.

"He's doing good work," the pastor said quietly.

Starr smiled.

"Yes, he is."

Pastor Barrett nodded thoughtfully.

"I knew he would."

For a moment, they both sat in silence.

Then Pastor Barrett closed his Bible slowly.

"Sometimes the most important thing a leader can do," he said, "is make sure the work continues after he's gone."

Starr felt the words settle deeply.

She remembered the scripture he had shown her weeks earlier.

A time to keep silent.

A time to speak.

For now, silence was still the right choice.

Later that night, after they returned home, Starr sat once again in the chair by the window.

The house was quiet.

Tyshawn worked in his office reviewing counseling notes from the empowerment group.

Jaunene slept upstairs.

Starr looked down at the Bible resting in her lap.

She turned again to Ecclesiastes.

"A time to keep silence, and a time to speak."

She closed the book gently.

Outside the window, the streetlight cast a soft glow across the quiet neighborhood.

Inside the house, everything felt peaceful.

But Starr knew something important.

The season was nearing its end.

And when the moment arrived, Tyshawn would need to be ready.

CHAPTER 16

The Pastor Falls

The Sunday morning service began like many others at City Life Church.

The sanctuary filled slowly with the quiet hum of conversation as members greeted one another and found their seats. Children slipped into the pews beside their parents. Ushers moved through the aisles handing out bulletins. The choir gathered near the front preparing for the opening hymn.

To most people, it felt like another ordinary Sunday.

But Starr noticed the small things.

She always did.

Pastor Barrett entered the sanctuary from the side hallway with his Bible in his hand. His smile was warm as always, and he greeted several members near the front before stepping behind the pulpit.

Yet something about the moment felt different.

His steps were careful.

Measured.

Starr watched closely from the pew where she sat beside Jaunene.

The choir began the first hymn, their voices filling the sanctuary with the familiar melody that had opened countless services over the years. The congregation stood together, the sound of voices rising in harmony beneath the tall ceiling of the church.

Tyshawn stood among the men from the empowerment group.

He noticed nothing unusual.

To him, Pastor Barrett looked like the same steady shepherd who had guided the church for decades.

When the hymn ended, Pastor Barrett stepped forward.

He rested his hands lightly on the pulpit and looked across the congregation.

For a moment he simply smiled.

"My brothers and sisters," he began, "this church has always believed in walking through life together."

His voice carried the same gentle authority it always had.

But Starr heard the difference.

A faint strain beneath the strength.

Pastor Barrett continued.

"We gather here each week not because life is easy… but because faith reminds us that we are never alone in our struggles."

Several members nodded quietly.

"We pray together. We cry together. And sometimes… we heal together."

His eyes moved across the sanctuary.

He saw the men from the empowerment group sitting together near the middle rows.

He saw the women who gathered weekly with Starr.

He saw families who had grown stronger through the honesty that had begun spreading through the church.

And he saw Tyshawn.

For a brief moment, their eyes met.

Pastor Barrett smiled softly.

Then he continued his sermon.

"Scripture reminds us that God works through ordinary people willing to serve."

His hand rested on the Bible that lay open before him.

"Sometimes that service comes through preaching."

He paused.

"And sometimes it comes through listening."

Several members of the congregation glanced toward Tyshawn.

Pastor Barrett continued speaking for several minutes.

But Starr saw the change first.

His voice slowed slightly.

His breathing deepened between sentences.

The hand resting on the pulpit tightened gently against the wood.

The congregation remained attentive.

No one else noticed.

Pastor Barrett reached the end of his message.

"And remember this," he said softly.

"Faith is not measured by how loudly we speak… but by how faithfully we serve."

He closed his Bible.

The congregation bowed their heads as he prepared to pray.

But before he could begin, Pastor Barrett paused.

His hand remained on the pulpit.

For a brief moment he seemed to steady himself.

Starr leaned forward slightly in her seat.

Tyshawn noticed her movement but did not understand why.

Pastor Barrett lifted his head again and smiled faintly.

"Let us pray—"

The words stopped.

His knees weakened.

And suddenly the sanctuary gasped as Pastor Barrett collapsed forward behind the pulpit.

Several people rushed forward immediately.

Tyshawn reached the front steps before most others.

"Pastor!"

The church fell into stunned silence.

Members stood frozen in the pews while the elders quickly gathered around him.

Someone called for an ambulance.

Another member began praying out loud.

Starr held Jaunene's hand tightly.

She had sensed that the moment was coming.

But even she was not prepared for how quickly it arrived.

Within minutes, the sound of sirens approached outside the church.

Paramedics entered the sanctuary and moved quickly to assist.

Tyshawn stepped back as they worked.

His heart pounded.

The man who had mentored him… guided him… ordained him… now lay motionless before the congregation he had served for so many years.

Starr placed her hand gently on Tyshawn's shoulder.

"It's going to be alright," she whispered.

But Tyshawn could barely hear her.

The sanctuary remained silent as the paramedics lifted Pastor Barrett onto the stretcher.

Members of the church began praying together quietly.

Some wept.

Others stood in stunned disbelief.

As the stretcher was carried down the center aisle, the congregation parted respectfully.

The church doors opened.

The ambulance lights flashed across the parking lot.

Tyshawn stood at the front of the sanctuary watching as they carried Pastor Barrett away.

The room that had once felt so full of life now felt painfully still.

And though no one spoke the words out loud yet, everyone in that sanctuary understood the truth.

A chapter in the life of City Life Church had just come to an end.

CHAPTER 17

Preparing the Greatest Funeral

The call came early the next morning.

Tyshawn had slept very little that night. The image of Pastor Barrett collapsing behind the pulpit replayed in his mind again and again. Even after the ambulance left the church, members had remained in the sanctuary praying late into the evening.

But sometime during the early hours of the morning, the hospital called.

Pastor Barrett had passed peacefully during the night.

For a long moment Tyshawn simply held the phone in silence.

Even though he had spent years directing funerals and standing beside families through their grief, this moment felt different.

This loss was personal.

He slowly lowered the phone and sat at the kitchen table.

The house was quiet.

Starr entered the room a few moments later. She could see the answer written on his face before he spoke.

“He’s gone,” Tyshawn said softly.

Starr nodded.

She placed her hand gently over his.

Jaunene stood quietly in the doorway, sensing the heaviness in the room even before she fully understood what had happened.

The church had lost its shepherd.

Later that morning Tyshawn drove to the funeral home.

The building looked the same as it always had. The same quiet lobby. The same soft lighting. The same arrangement room where he had helped countless families prepare services for their loved ones.

But today he walked through the doors carrying the weight of preparing the funeral for the man who had mentored him.

His staff greeted him gently.

“We heard the news,” one of them said quietly.

Tyshawn nodded.

“The church will want to hold the service there,” another staff member added.

“They will.”

Tyshawn walked slowly into the preparation room.

For a moment he simply stood there.

Every funeral director understands that some services carry a deeper emotional weight than others.

This would be the most important service he had ever directed.

Not because of the size of the crowd.

But because of the life being honored.

He sat down at the arrangement table and opened a notebook.

The service would need to reflect Pastor Barrett's life.

His leadership.

His compassion.

His faith.

Later that afternoon the phone began ringing.

Church members called.

Community leaders called.

Pastors from neighboring churches called.

Everyone wanted to know the same thing.

"When will the service be held?"

Tyshawn spoke calmly to each person.

"City Life Church will host the service."

"The date will be Saturday morning."

"The entire community is welcome."

By evening the church parking lot had filled again.

Members gathered quietly inside the sanctuary.

Some prayed.

Some simply sat in silence.

Starr moved gently among the people offering comfort.

The women from her ministry stood beside one another, many of them remembering how Pastor Barrett had supported the work they had begun.

Across the room the men from the empowerment group gathered near the front pews.

James spoke first.

"We should help however we can."

Another man nodded.

"He stood by us when we needed someone."

Several others agreed.

"We'll serve as pallbearers."

"And we should stand together during the service."

Tyshawn overheard the conversation as he entered the sanctuary.

For a moment he simply watched them.

These were men who once struggled even to speak openly.

Now they stood together ready to honor the man who helped guide them toward healing.

Starr approached quietly.

"The church is ready to help," she said softly.

Tyshawn nodded.

"I want the service to reflect his life."

"It will," Starr replied.

She looked around the sanctuary.

The pews were filled with people who had been touched by Pastor Barrett's ministry.

The men whose lives had changed.

The women whose families had grown stronger.

The children who had grown up hearing his sermons.

"He built something special here," Starr said.

Tyshawn looked toward the pulpit.

"Yes he did."

The planning continued late into the evening.

Music selections were discussed.

Scriptures were chosen.

Community leaders asked to speak.

By the time the final plans were completed, one thing had become clear.

This would not be an ordinary funeral.

It would be the greatest service City Life Church had ever seen.

And Tyshawn would be the one responsible for guiding it.

CHAPTER 18

The Greatest Funeral at City Life Church

Saturday morning arrived slowly.

Before the sun had fully risen, cars were already turning into the parking lot at City Life Church. The morning air carried a quiet stillness, but the church grounds were beginning to fill with people who had come from across the city and beyond.

By eight o'clock the parking lot was nearly full.

By nine o'clock cars lined the street in both directions.

People continued arriving.

Pastors from neighboring churches stepped out of their vehicles dressed in dark suits. Families who had moved away years earlier returned to honor the man who had once guided their lives. Members of the community who had never attended City Life Church still felt compelled to come because they had heard the stories of Pastor Barrett's compassion.

Inside the sanctuary, soft music was played while people found their seats.

The casket rested at the front of the church beneath the large wooden cross that hung above the pulpit. White flowers surrounded the platform in simple arrangements that reflected Pastor Barrett's humble nature.

Tyshawn stood near the front doors greeting people as they entered.

One by one they shook his hand.

"I'm sorry for your loss."

"He was a good man."

"He changed my life."

Tyshawn nodded respectfully to each person.

Even with years of experience directing services, this moment felt overwhelming.

This was not just another funeral.

This was the farewell to the man who had mentored him, believed in him, and prepared him for the work he now carried.

Starr stood near the front of the sanctuary helping guide people to their seats. Her calm presence helped steady the emotions filling the room.

Jaunene sat quietly beside several younger children who had gathered near the side pews. She spoke softly to them, helping them understand why the room felt so heavy.

By the time the service began, the sanctuary was completely full.

Additional chairs had been placed along the back wall.

Some people stood in the hallways.

Others watched through the open doors.

The choir rose slowly.

Their voices lifted a familiar hymn that echoed through the sanctuary.

Many in the congregation sang softly through tears.

When the song ended, Tyshawn walked slowly toward the pulpit.

The room felt completely silent.

For a moment, he simply stood there.

Looking out across the sea of faces.

Faces filled with grief.

Faces filled with gratitude.

Faces filled with memories.

He took a slow breath.

“Pastor Barrett spent his life walking beside people,” he began quietly.

His voice carried through the sanctuary.

“He stood with families during their hardest moments.”

“He listened when people felt no one else would.”

"He believed that healing begins when people tell the truth about their lives."

Tyshawn paused.

His eyes moved across the congregation.

"Many of us sitting in this room today are here because he helped us find hope when we thought it was gone."

Several members wiped tears from their faces.

Tyshawn stepped away from the pulpit.

"This service is not only about mourning his passing," he continued.

"It is about honoring the life he lived."

He nodded toward the front row.

"The men from the empowerment group would like to share a few words."

James stood first.

He walked slowly to the front of the sanctuary.

Behind him, the other men from the group rose and followed.

Instead of sitting in their seats, they surrounded the casket.

Not as pallbearers.

As brothers.

James spoke quietly.

"When I first came to this church, I didn't know how to talk about my pain."

He glanced at the men beside him.

"Pastor Barrett didn't force us to speak."

"He simply created a place where honesty was welcome."

Another man stepped forward.

"My family nearly fell apart before I found this church."

He looked toward the congregation.

"Because of Pastor Barrett… and because of the ministry that grew here… my children still have their father."

One by one the men shared brief testimonies.

The sanctuary remained silent as their voices filled the room.

Then the women stood.

Starr remained seated.

She had never led the group publicly.

But the women she had guided stepped forward together.

Danielle spoke first.

"My husband found courage in this church before he died."

Her voice trembled slightly.

"Pastor Barrett gave him that chance."

Another woman spoke about how her marriage had been restored.

Another thanked the church for helping her understand the pain her husband had carried silently for years.

The testimonies continued.

Each one revealed another life touched by the ministry Pastor Barrett had built.

After the final speaker returned to their seat, the choir rose again.

Their voices filled the sanctuary with a song of faith and hope.

Tyshawn stepped forward one last time.

He walked slowly toward the casket.

For a moment he rested his hand gently on the polished wood.

Then he turned toward the congregation.

"Pastor Barrett once told me something I will never forget."

The room listened carefully.

"He said the most powerful sermons are not always spoken from the pulpit."

Tyshawn paused.

"Sometimes the most powerful sermon is the life someone lives."

His voice softened.

"And today… this church is the sermon he left behind."

The congregation rose to their feet.

The service ended in quiet reverence.

Outside the church, the crowd continued to gather as the pallbearers prepared to carry the casket.

The men from the empowerment group stood together at the front steps.

Starr watched from the doorway beside Tyshawn.

Neither of them spoke.

But both understood something important.

The man who had led the church for decades was gone.

Yet the work he began was still alive.

And now it was their responsibility to carry it forward.

CHAPTER 19

The Reading of the Will

The days following Pastor Barrett's funeral passed in a quiet blur.

City Life Church remained busy. Members continued gathering for prayer. The ministries that Pastor Barrett had supported continued meeting, though the atmosphere carried a softer tone as the congregation adjusted to his absence.

The empowerment group still met on Wednesday evenings.

The Women of the Window still gathered around Starr.

But every conversation eventually returned to the same thought.

Pastor Barrett was gone.

One afternoon, a letter arrived addressed Tyshawn.

It came from a local attorney who had handled many of the church's legal matters over the years. The message was brief, asking Tyshawn to come by the office the following morning regarding Pastor Barrett's estate.

Tyshawn sat at the kitchen table reading the letter again.

Starr poured two cups of tea and placed one beside him.

“You knew this would come eventually,” she said gently.

Tyshawn nodded.

“I just didn’t expect it to feel this strange.”

Jaunene sat at the end of the table, quietly finishing her homework. She looked up when she heard them speaking.

“Are you going back to the church tomorrow?” She asked.

“Not the church,” Tyshawn replied. “The lawyer’s office.”

Jaunene nodded thoughtfully and returned to her notebook.

The next morning Tyshawn arrived at the attorney’s office downtown.

The building was small but familiar. Pastor Barrett had handled many of the church’s official matters there through the years.

The receptionist greeted him kindly.

“They’re expecting you.”

Tyshawn stepped into the office where the attorney waited behind a large wooden desk.

“Thank you for coming,” the man said warmly.

Tyshawn sat down.

"I understand Pastor Barrett left instructions that needed to be shared with you."

The attorney opened a folder and removed a sealed envelope.

"This letter was written personally by Pastor Barrett."

Tyshawn held the envelope for a moment before opening it.

Inside was a single handwritten page.

The familiar handwriting immediately brought back memories of the pastor's sermons and handwritten notes.

Tyshawn began reading silently.

Tyshawn,

If you are reading this letter, then the time has come for the church to continue the work that God has placed before it.

For many years, the funeral home has served this community during its most painful moments. I have always believed that comforting families during grief is a sacred responsibility.

You have shown the heart for that responsibility.

Tyshawn paused briefly before continuing.

Your work with grieving families, your studies in psychology and grief counseling, and the compassion you have shown through the empowerment ministry have convinced me that you are prepared to continue this work.

For that reason, I have left the ownership of the funeral home in your care.

Tyshawn lowered the letter slowly.

The attorney nodded.

“Pastor Barrett made this decision some time ago.”

“He believed you were the right person to continue the ministry connected to the funeral home.”

Tyshawn sat quietly.

The responsibility felt enormous.

He had spent years working there.

But owning it was something different.

“Is the church aware of this?” Tyshawn asked.

“The church board was informed,” the attorney replied. “They supported his decision.”

Tyshawn folded the letter carefully and placed it back into the envelope.

Later that afternoon he returned home.

Starr was sitting in the chair by the window reading when he entered.

She looked up.

"How did it go?"

Tyshawn handed her the letter.

She read it slowly.

When she finished, she looked at him with a calm smile.

"He trusted you."

Tyshawn sat down across from her.

"It feels like a lot to carry."

Starr closed the letter and placed it gently on the table.

"You've already been carrying it for years," she said.

"The difference now is simply that everyone else can see it."

Jaunene walked into the room just then.

"Did the lawyer tell you something important?" She asked.

Tyshawn nodded.

"He did."

"What kind of important?"

Tyshawn thought for a moment before answering.

"Pastor Barrett left me the funeral home."

Jaunene's eyes widened slightly.

"That's a big responsibility."

Tyshawn smiled.

"Yes, it is."

She nodded thoughtfully.

Then she returned quietly to her room.

Starr looked at Tyshawn again.

"Are you ready?"

Tyshawn glanced toward the window.

Outside the evening light was fading slowly across the neighborhood.

He thought about the church.

The families he had helped through grief.

The empowerment group.

The ordination.

The legacy Pastor Barrett had left behind.

Then he nodded.

"Yes."

For the first time since the funeral, the future felt clear.

And the work was only just the beginning.

CHAPTER 20

The Legacy

Spring arrived slowly that year.

The trees surrounding City Life Church began filling with new leaves, and the cold quiet of winter gradually gave way to warmer mornings. Yet even as the seasons changed, the memory of Pastor Barrett still rested gently over the church.

For many members, his absence was felt most on Sunday mornings.

The sanctuary looked the same.

The cross still hung above the pulpit.

The choir still sang familiar hymns.

But the man who had stood behind that pulpit for decades was no longer there.

Still, the church had not grown silent.

It had grown stronger.

Tyshawn now spent many of his mornings moving between the funeral home and the church. The responsibilities left to him by Pastor Barrett had become part of his daily life.

At the funeral home he continued guiding families through grief with the same compassion he had always shown.

At the church he worked closely with the leadership, serving in the role of Associate Pastor of Pastoral Care. His focus remained exactly where Pastor Barrett had believed it belonged—helping people navigate the painful seasons of life.

Grief.

Loss.

Healing.

The empowerment group continued meeting each Wednesday evening.

The circle of chairs had grown larger.

New men arrived almost every week, often invited by someone who had already found courage within the group.

The conversation remained honest.

Sometimes difficult.

But it's always hopeful.

Across town, Starr's ministry continued growing as well.

Women gathered faithfully around her guidance, learning how to support their husbands while also caring for their own emotional and spiritual strength.

Starr never tried to place herself at the center of the ministry.

She simply listened.

Asked thoughtful questions.

And reminded the women that healing required patience.

Often, she returned home late on Wednesday nights and sat quietly in the chair by the window.

The chair had become more than just a place to rest.

It had become the place where she reflected on everything happening around them.

Tyshawn often worked in his office down the hallway reviewing counseling notes or preparing meetings at the church.

And somewhere between those two spaces, their daughter quietly observed everything.

Jaunene turned thirteen that spring.

She had grown taller, more thoughtful.

The notebook she carried with her had slowly filled with ideas.

One afternoon she sat at the kitchen table while Tyshawn reviewed a stack of papers nearby.

"What are you writing?" he asked.

Jaunene looked up.

"Just some ideas."

"For school?"

She shook her head.

"For church."

Tyshawn leaned back in his chair.

"What kind of ideas?"

Jaunene turned the notebook toward him.

At the top of the page she had written carefully:

Helping Kids Understand Life

Tyshawn smiled softly.

"What would that look like?"

She shrugged slightly.

"Kids hear things too."

"Hear what?"

"When grown-ups are sad."

"When people die."

"When families are struggling."

Tyshawn nodded slowly.

“That’s true.”

“They don’t always understand it though,” Jaunene continued.

“Someone should help them.”

Tyshawn looked at Starr sitting quietly in the chair by the window.

She was watching the conversation with a gentle smile.

“You might be right,” he said.

Jaunene closed the notebook.

“Maybe one day.”

Later that month another important moment arrived.

Tyshawn walked across the stage of the university auditorium dressed in a black academic gown.

Rows of graduates sat beside him as families filled the seats of the large hall.

Starr and Jaunene sat together near the front of the audience.

When Tyshawn’s name was called, he stood and walked across the stage.

The announcer spoke clearly.

“Doctor of Psychology.”

Starr wiped a quiet tear from her eye as the audience applauded.

Years of work had led to that moment.

His studies had focused deeply on grief, counseling, and the human experience of loss—areas of study often connected to the field of thanatology.

The knowledge would only deepen the work he was already doing every day.

After the ceremony, the three of them walked slowly across the campus courtyard.

Jaunene looked up at him proudly.

"So now you're a doctor?"

Tyshawn laughed.

"I guess so."

"Does that mean you know everything now?"

"Not even close."

Starr smiled.

"That's why he'll keep learning."

As they reached the parking lot, Tyshawn paused for a moment.

He looked up toward the sky.

A quiet sense of gratitude settled over him.

Pastor Barrett had once told him that ministry was not about standing above people.

It was about walking beside them.

Now the work is continuing.

Back home that evening, Starr sat again in the chair by the window.

The soft glow of the streetlight reflected across the glass.

Tyshawn worked quietly in his office.

Jaunene sat at the table writing in her notebook again.

The house felt peaceful.

But the future was already beginning to take shape.

The ministries that had begun around a kitchen table had grown into something far larger than anyone expected.

And now, without anyone fully realizing it yet, a new chapter was quietly forming.

Jaunene closed her notebook and looked toward her parents.

One day she would understand everything she had witnessed.

The grief.

The healing.

The strength of faith.

But for now, she simply watched it.

Learning.

Preparing.

Because the legacy Pastor Barrett began…
the ministry Tyshawn and Starr carried forward…

was only just the beginning.

ABOUT THE AUTHOR

Shawn E. Wells, LFD, BCCC, CGC, is a Licensed Funeral Director, Board Certified Christian Counselor, and Certified Grief Counselor whose work focuses on helping individuals and families navigate grief, faith, and life's most significant transitions.

Through years of professional service in funeral care and counseling education, Wells has witnessed firsthand the emotional, spiritual, and practical decisions individuals and families face during moments of loss and uncertainty. His work emphasizes clarity, responsibility, and compassionate understanding when people are confronted with life's most difficult crossroads.

These experiences contributed to the development of **ENROUTE-RX**, a structured framework designed to guide individuals through major life decisions using disciplined evaluation, credential literacy, emotional awareness, and faith-based reflection. The ENROUTE-RX framework encourages thoughtful decision-making rather than reaction during moments of grief, legal responsibility, financial pressure, or personal transition.

Wells' exploration of these ideas first appeared in *Funeral Service at a Crossroads*, an examination of the modern funeral profession addressing industry reform, regulatory oversight, economic pressure, and the preservation of professional dignity. As the scope of that work expanded beyond industry structure into broader questions of grief literacy, identity, professional responsibility, and eternal perspective, it developed into the broader body of **ENROUTE-RX writings**, including:

ENROUTE-RX
The foundational framework introducing structured evaluation and credential literacy for navigating life transitions.

ENROUTE-RX: Crossroads
A disciplined question-and-answer guide for individuals and professionals facing grief, legal responsibility, financial decisions, and identity reconstruction.
ENROUTE-RX: At the Crossroads of Eternity
An exploration of mortality, faith, and eternal accountability within the context of life's decisive moments.

In addition to his professional and educational writing, Wells also developed the **EnRoute-Rx narrative series**, which presents the emotional and spiritual realities of grief, healing, faith, and family through storytelling.

Beginning with *Sunday in a Truck* and continuing with *The Chair by the Window*, the series explores how conversations, community, and faith help individuals and families navigate the hidden struggles that often accompany grief and life transitions. The story will continue with a forthcoming third volume that follows Jaunene as she begins discovering her own calling to help children understand grief, faith, and life.

Across both his professional work and narrative storytelling, Wells maintains a consistent principle:

Clarity precedes stability.

Through education, counseling insight, and faith-centered reflection, his work encourages readers to approach life's most important crossroads with wisdom, compassion, and disciplined understanding.

What Comes Next

The story of City Life Church is not finished.

Jaunene has spent years watching the conversations happening around her. She has listened quietly as men and women learned how to speak honestly about pain, grief, and faith.

Now she begins asking her own questions.

What about the children who hear those conversations but do not understand them?

What about the young hearts learning about loss for the first time?

In the next chapter of the EnRoute-Rx journey, Jaunene begins discovering her own calling—helping children understand life, grief, and faith in ways that give them hope.

The journey continues.

Acknowledgments

Every book is the result of encouragement, patience, and the support of people who believe in the message behind the story.

I want to express sincere gratitude to my daughter Starr, whose wisdom, encouragement, and dedication to counseling helped strengthen the vision behind EnRoute-Rx. Walking through the counseling certification journey together was one of the most meaningful experiences of my life.

I am also grateful to my Aunt Eva, whose constant encouragement and willingness to listen to every idea helped push this work forward. Many of the conversations that shaped these pages began during those long discussions.

Finally, I thank every reader who opens this book and allows the message of compassion, faith, and healing to continue spreading.

The journey continues.

For years, Jaunene listened quietly.

She listened from the staircase.
She listened from the hallway.
She listened while the adults spoke about grief, faith, healing, and the burdens people carried in silence.

She watched her father help broken men find their voice.
She watched her mother help families understand what the heart often struggles to explain.

Now she is beginning to understand something for herself.

Some people are called to help the grieving.

Some people are called to guide the hurting.

And some are called to help the next generation understand both.

Jaunene is just beginning her journey.

And the story is not finished.

www.ingramcontent.com/pod-product-compliance
Lightning Source LLC
LaVergne TN
LVHW010914110826
845149LV00013B/2356

* 9 7 9 8 9 9 4 6 3 0 9 6 9 *